# THE
# SNUFF TAKERS
# EPHEMERIS

# VOLUME EIGHT:
# DEAD BY DAWN

# ON THE COVER

## My Intentions Are War by Rob Jones
### Ink and Acrylic on Found Wood, 2010. 22" x 30"

### ABOUT THE SUBJECT

Lord Invader (Dec. 13, 1914 - Oct. 15, 1961), also known as Rupert Westmore Grant, was a Trinidad-born Calypso singer who achieved some measure of fame internationally for co-writing the original version of "Rum and Coca Cola," a major wartime hit for the Andrews Sisters in 1945. Grant wrote the lyrics, which were set to a musical accompaniment written by Lionel Belasco.

"Rum and Coca Cola" was a well-known song in the isle of Trinidad, even though it was never formally recorded. While stationed there as an NCO, actor Morey Amsterdam (*The Dick Van Dyke Show*, American International's series of *Beach Party* movies from the 1960's) heard it performed live on stage and jotted down the lyrics and chorus, and quickly copyrighted the catchy tune in the US. It was recorded by the Andrews Sisters and reached #1 on the Pop charts.

When Lord Invader heard the Andrews Sister's version on the radio, he packed up and headed to New York to sue for copyright infringement. During the two-year legal battle, Invader recorded a handful of session singles and a few live performances, which were produced by folk musician archivist Alan Lomax. Finally, in 1948, Invader received massive royalties from "Rum and Coca-Cola," and he was awarded the copyright to it, which he shared with Lionel Belasco. (Morey Amsterdam was also awarded a separate copyright for his slightly revised version, which contained lyrics that differed from the original.)

Invader stayed behind in New York, and began writing folk songs about civil rights and segregation. He died in 1961 from a mysterious heart attack, still the subject of debate today by Calypso historians.

### ABOUT THE ARTIST

Rob Jones was born and raised in Ashland, OH. He earned a Bachelor of Arts in Studio Art from Kent State University in 1998, after which he moved to Columbus, OH. He has since earned his teaching certificate from Ashland University and is currently working on earning his Master Degree. Rob has been teaching elementary art for Olentangy Schools since 2007.

Rob started showing work locally in the fall of 1998 and has had exhibitions in many bars and restaurants throughout Columbus. He has participated in several local group shows in addition to his recent, (second) one-man show in Louisiana in the spring of 2012.

Rob's art focuses on a growing appreciation and respect for the Blues and its history. His art is created in a manner similar to that of the instruments and art of blues musicians and folk artist who inspire him. Musicians such as Abner Jay and Super Chikan who made instruments out of anything from discarded jawbones of livestock to cigar boxes, and folk artists such as Son Thomas and William Hawkins who created art by using mud, homemade clay, cardboard, and wood. Rob uses found wood, old fences, bottle caps, scraps of metal and other salvaged artifacts to tell stories. The found materials bring their own history and add a genuine earthiness to the art and reflect the character of his subjects.

Rob lives in Columbus with his wife and two sons. You can find his art at the following places:

*Current work at:* robjonesfolkart.blogspot.com
*Older work at:* popdenial.blogspot.com
*Much Older work at:* artwanted.com/popdenial

© 2013, Lucien Publishing.

**THE SNUFF TAKER'S EPHEMERIS** is published sporadically by Lucien Publishing, Fayetteville NC. Volume Eight, Spring 2013. Cost: 10.99/single volume; 43.96/per year. Address: PO Box 287, Spring Lake, NC 28390. www.STephemeris.com.

Advertising and distribution/bulk purchase queries: distribution@STephemeris.com.

ISBN-13: 978-0-9854781-4-8

ISBN-10: 0985478144

## STAFF

### EDITORS

**RW Hubbard**
*President, Punisher*

**Mick Hellwig**
*Editor in Chief*

**Micah Rimel**
*Managing Editor*

### WRITERS

Gillian Bromley

Seth Desjardins

Anthony Haddad

Simon Handelsman

Mick Hellwig

RW Hubbard

Bill Johnson

Nigel McCarren

Micah Rimel

David Thigpen

James Walter

Larry Waters

# Contents

**THIS ISSUE DEDICATED TO** Marcus Carlsson, who stepped up to the plate when no one else did. Cheers.

**SPECIAL THANKS:** Matt Slate, Steve Abbott, Marcus Carlsson, Niklas Trieb, Tara Armstrong, Talya Carroll, Chad & Nash, David (Mr. Snuff), Elisha Cozine (our Chief Photographer), Brant Comstock, Nigel McCarron, Mark and Patrick Vogel, and everyone we forgot, plus our faithful readership.

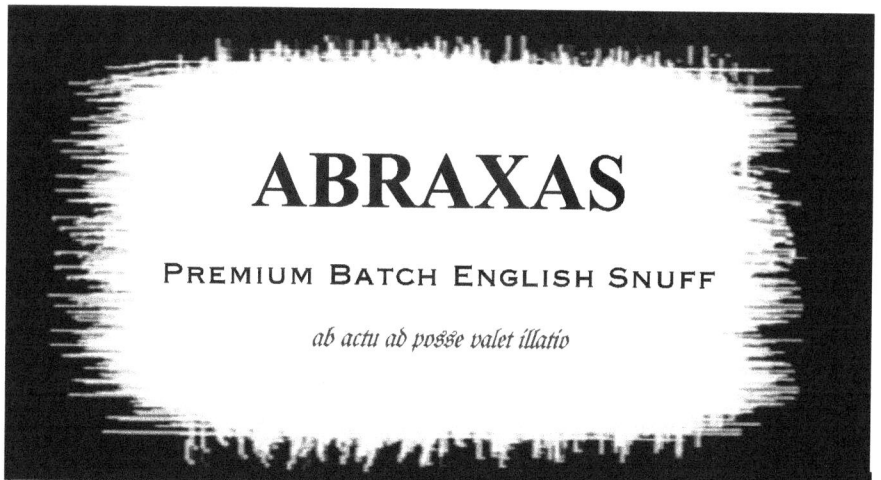

# Note From The President

When I got the new billing sheet in the other day I was surprised to find that we were being carried in about 500 stores nationwide called "KM-S." I had to call around to find out who KM-S was, and it turned out to be **K-Mart/Sears.** Take *that*, Wal-Mart!

I had to pause and reflect upon the happy memories I had as a youth tagging along with my parents to K-Mart to look over the latest **Masters of the Universe figures.** For years K-Mart was the only player in town when it came to chain department stores. Then the first Wal-Mart opened up in 1988 and it seemed that within hours, K-Mart was gone, replaced by a Flea Market. I remember my dad getting a shopping cart full of Mopar-branded 10w-40 oil quarts that had been reduced to 20 cents or so during the store closing.

I still see an occasional K-Mart here and there. And yes, I'm talking about the *real* K-Mart, not this "Big K" superstore crap that they've had on life support for the last ten years. Sadly, all the K-Marts I come across always look deserted, even during the middle of the day. Who knows, maybe our magazine will bring shoppers back in droves. (Stop laughing; it could happen!)

Shop smart, shop K-Mart!

RW Hubbard

***Corrections and Retractions-*** *Just the facts: In Volume 6, we stated that Jack Webb died of lung cancer. In fact, he suffered a major heart attack while getting up out of his chair to change the channel on his television. At the time of his death, he was chain-smoking 4 to 5 packs of L & M Cigarettes (his latest sponsor) a day.*

***Late Breaking News:*** *As we were going to print, we learned that the semi-annual price hike that American tobacco companies regularly implement will go in to effect starting Mid-June. First on the block is Phillip Morris; other manufacturers are expected to follow suit shortly thereafter.*

# Editorial

## SMOKELESS TOBACCO, HISTORY AND THINGS YOUR MOM SAYS

Since time immemorial (or, at least 1753-onwards) Americans have enjoyed, used and, in some cases, become synonymous with smokeless tobacco. British authors from the earliest periods describe Americans as plug tobacco chewin', spittin', angsty sailor-types itching for a fight against anybody, anytime, anywhere. Really, it's all there (truth be told, the British weren't too fond of Americans after the French and Indian war or Seven Years war as some of you may know). Why was the American habit of chewing tobacco so recklessly targeted? Propaganda, for one, and pure military need.

On fighting ships of the time (British) tobacco chewing was an acceptable practice; as long as no spit stayed on deck. American ships were a little more lax, and much of this had to do with ship design.

British vessels were square rigged ungainly things; their sole purpose was to serve as a mobile platform for a series of very heavy, large caliber guns. One of the chief duties of British seaman was to make the deck smooth and uniform, thus allowing free recoil of guns that fired 9 lb. shot to 34 lb carronades that served to make the enemy gravely wounded at close range. Tobacco spit on a huge British ship, due to its viscosity and nascent prevalence , could impact the way a gun recoiled (i.e. skewing it from its expected reverse trajectory. This was a real problem, in those days of wooden carriage guns, and captains forbade the 'spitting upon the deck' early on, as lives and oftentimes limbs were lost, as these huge cannons went astray from their accustomed recoil. A small amount of lubricitive tobacco was truly a matter of life and death for those early sailors.

American ships, on the other hand, were quite accustomed to spitting anywhere they pleased upon the decks of their ships of service. American ships were also, by and large, vessels of shallow draft and of schooner type (the Americans invented what would eventually be known as the 'schooner'- the British schooner was little more than a Cutter with lateen sails), meaning they drew a great deal of water. This water, the sea, flushed almost all of the American's tobacco effluvium along side the ship and did not interfere with the working of the guns (most of which were shipped below decks at the time).

The point is that tobacco 'spit' had a combat impact upon the two most powerful naval forces at the time. If only Swedish snus or nasal snuff been more predominant amongst sailors of that particular era, history could have been rewritten.

Snuff, er... stuff to think about. You writers out there, give us your alternate histories! Or at least weigh an anchor in on the subject. Your thoughts are noticed and appreciated.

Till then, Achors A-weigh!

Micah Roimel

Managing Editor,
Carouser

# Ephemera!

A little-known provision in the Affordable Healthcare Act (affectionately referred to as Obamacare by pundits and supporters alike) could have a drastic impact on the income of tobacco users.

Buried inconspicuously in the middle of the nearly 3,000 page tome is a clause that is just now starting to make headlines. The provision allows insurers to charge up to 50% more in premiums for users of tobacco or nicotine. Depending upon a person's annual income, insurance costs can account for approximately 20% of their income if they use nicotine products.

"I thought this was supposed to be the Affordable Healthcare Act?" asked student Brian Moore of Fayetteville State University. Moore, who uses Camel snus, can expect to be charged 1/10th of his annual income in insurance costs. He is not eligible for subsidized insurance deductions since he is enrolled another government program that does not allow "double dipping," or utilizing two federal subsides at the same time.

On top of that, insurance companies can still refuse to cover tobacco-related illnesses, even if the insured has never used tobacco in his life. Said Meyer Langmen, a political science teacher at the school, "The way the law is written right now is that if a person checks into the hospital with oral cancer or lung cancer, the insurance company can deny coverage based on the assumption that the patient is a tobacco user, even if that assumption is false. In most ways, the AFA is the single worst thing to happen to uninsured tobacco users, or those with symptoms of tobacco-related disease, simply because they're completely left out of any sort of medical help for their problems."

He further went on to explain that "Nicotine addiction is a pre-existing condition, and this law is supposed to help those people rather than punish them. Some companies will try to veer their customers towards pharmaceutical alternatives, but since these medications contain nicotine, [the person using NRT treatments such as nicotine patches, lozenges or gum] will still be charged the same rate as the two-pack-a-day smoker, even if that person has been tobacco-free for years. There's really no way to determine whether a person is a snuffer or a chewer of nicotine gum just by a simple blood test."

Contrarily, cigar smokers that suffer higher rates of oral and throat cancers than smokeless tobacco users will likely be unaffected by the new law. "Occasional cigar smokers don't usually test positive for nicotine," according to Langmen. "So even though they're at a higher risk for health problems than smokeless tobacco users, they're not going to be held accountable for their actions."

The one silver lining in this cloud of discrimination is another clause that allows each individual state to pick or choose the tobacco premium increase, which means that traditional anti-tobacco areas such as the Northeast will probably adopt the clause while pro-tobacco states such as Ohio and the Carolinas will probably pass on it. "Of course, this is all speculation at this point," Langmen added. "We won't know until each state ratifies its version of the law."

Langmen suggests urging your local congressman to vote against any sort of heavy premiums for tobacco users. "Worst case scenario is that if your state passes the law with the tobacco clause, you can move to a state that voted against it. Otherwise, you can opt to pay for the higher premiums or opt out of the system altogether, which will cost you roughly the same as the higher premiums. Either way, tobacco users are getting the short end of the stick here."

# ...Presenting all the news that's fit to reprint...

## Russia Attempts to Ban Smokeless Tobacco

Russian Parliament has passed a law to ban the use, sale and possession of all smokeless tobacco. This includes the use of snus, snuff, Indian-style guthka, and Western style plug or rope tobacco. In fact, the bill plainly states that "if it is tobacco that is not set on fire in order to be consumed, then it is deemed illegal under our guidelines."

Alexi Nadhezdhin, Minister of Health, falsely claims that smokeless tobacco is more dangerous than smoking and that most tobacco users are minors. Although smokeless tobacco use is relatively minor compared to other countries, Russia's cigarette companies have backed the law, presumably to protect their own assets.

The bill still needs to be approved by the Prime Minister before it becomes law. Let's hope that for snuff and snus users, this proposed law never goes through.

## FDA Appeal Shut Down by Federal Appeals Court

Washington DC's Sixth Circuit court shot down the FDA's request to rehear their case for graphic warning pictures on cigarette packs.

The court declared the warning labels, which featured such graphic examples as diseased lungs and rotted mouths, unconstitutional under the USA's First Amendment, as well as being misleading and inaccurate.

The states that initially backed the FDA's appeal include Alaska, Arizona, Arkansas, California, Connecticut, Hawaii, Illinois, Iowa, Maine, Maryland, Mississippi, Montana, New Hampshire, New Mexico, Ohio, Rhode Island, South Dakota, Utah, Vermont, Washington and West Virginia.

## British American Tobacco elects former White House Physician Richard Tubb as Director

Brigadier General (retired) Dr Richard Tubb, a U.S. citizen, has been appointed a Non-Executive Director of British American Tobacco p.l.c with effect from 28th January 2013.

As one of the longest serving White House physicians, Dr Tubb's leadership spanned more than 14 years and served the Administrations of Presidents Clinton, Bush and Obama. By the time he retired from the White House in 2009, he had served as Director, White House Medical Unit, Physician to the White House, and Physician to the President.

Dr Tubb is a leading public health figure actively involved in the science and policy development of tobacco harm reduction and alternative nicotine products.

Commenting on his appointment, Richard Burrows, Chairman of British American Tobacco p.l.c., said: "I am delighted to be welcoming such a prominent and well respected expert in the field of tobacco harm reduction to our Board. This appointment further demonstrates our commitment to putting science at the heart of our business and I am excited about the role Richard will play in the development of our strategy."

## Cigarette Smoking Declines In South Korea

Cigarette Smoking declined by almost 8% between 2011 and 2012 according to an industry survey.

The decline was blamed on financial conditions, public smoking bans and smokers switching to smoke-free alternatives such as e-cigs and snuff.

# Ephemera

## Smokeless Lounge Opens in Bloomington, MN

In what may be a precursor to an emerging new trend, a "smokeless smoke lounge" opened its doors in Minnesota recently.

Mimicking a traditional cigar bar, the Smokeless Smoking sells a wide variety of electronic cigarette items and offers a lounge area for "vapers" to relax and chat, watch television or play video games.

Although there is no tobacco sold or used on the lounge premises, Bloomington, MN requires Smokeless Smoking to have a tobacco license, and the company does pay tobacco taxes on products that contain nicotine. Still, there was clearly a need for "a clubhouse for people who like electronic cigarettes," said the owner.

## Swedish Match North America Rolls Back Prices on Timberwolf, Longhorn After Introduction of Catch Lids

**RICHMOND, Va.,** Jan. 14, 2013- Swedish Match announced today that the company is reducing the factory selling price for all Longhorn and Timber Wolf pouches to $.90. The new list price represents a 31% reduction for Longhorn and a 49% reduction for Timber Wolf. The new pricing goes into effect on Monday, January 21, 2013.

"Historically, the 'pouch' segment of the moist snuff category has grown at twice the rate of the total category," according to Joe Ackerman, Marketing Director of US Smokeless Brands. "Within the last year that rate has accelerated to 3 times the category rate. We anticipate this growth trend to continue as tobacco consumers continue to gravitate towards the convenience of pouch products."

The pricing change comes on the heels of the introduction of Timber Wolf and Longhorn's new unique package design that offers the disposable pouch compartment - standard issue for Swedish snus portion brands, but heretofore unseen on American smokeless products.

Ackerman adds, "We not only feel that our pricing decision delivers strong value to consumers, but also contributes to robust category growth. Additionally with the recent pouch packaging change, consumers will successfully differentiate Timber Wolf & Longhorn Pouches from competitive brands."

## British Columbia Spends Almost 20 Million Dollars in Taxpayer's Money to Hand Out Free Chantix and Zyban

While the Ministry of Health in British Columbia has ramped up efforts to ban the use of smokeless tobacco products and electronic cigarettes, they have also partnered up with Pfizer Inc. to give out free Chantix (as well as other smoke cessation drugs from different pharmaceutical companies) to smokers who wish to quit.

Conveniently sidestepping the fact that Pfizer is in the middle of several class action lawsuits filed by victims of the drug's side effects, the Ministry of Health acknowledged the controversy but added that "There has been no impact on the program, though we are aware of the class-action lawsuit and are keeping up-to-date with any new information. We will continue to monitor for new information and will adjust the program as necessary." Next year's tax money allotment for this program is earmarked for 15-25 million dollars, "depending on interest."

## Proposed Legislation in Three States Would Prohibit Welfare Recipients From Buying Tobacco

Virginia, Alabama and Texas have all recently introduced similar bills that would try to prohibit welfare recipients from using state-provided funds to purchase alcohol, tobacco and lap dances.

Noting that most welfare recipients in their states use taxpayer money to buy alcohol, tobacco and "a night out at the strip club," Senators from the three states have created a convoluted plan that would block benefit recipients from withdrawing money on their EBT cards from ATMs located near businesses that sold alcohol or tobacco, or from businesses that featured "live, nude entertainers."

Even among supporters of welfare reform, the bills have garnered little backing. The problem is that they are almost impossible to enforce. One congressman noted that "If a benefit recipient is withdrawing cash to buy food, and that ATM is located in a supermarket that sells cigarettes or beer, then the recipient will not be able to access their funds to buy what the benefits are intended for. Conversely, if they wanted to buy beer or cigarettes badly enough, they could just go to another ATM that isn't barred from use by the state."

A more effective way to bar welfare recipients from spending taxpayer dollars on booze and tobacco would be to have them voluntarily submit to monthly drug tests to determine whether or not they use alcohol or nicotine. If they test positive for either substance, their funding would be cut. Of course, there's still no test that would determine whether or not that person has received a lap dance within the last 30 days...

## Discriminatory Bill Introduced Into South Carolina Legislature

South Carolina, one of the few states in the country that actually has laws in place barring discrimination against employees that use tobacco, has been served a bill that would attempt to repeal that law.

Section 41-1-85 of the 1976 SC Legal Code prohibits employers from taking personnel actions based on the use of tobacco products outside the workplace. Employers are not allowed to even *ask* their employees whether or not they use tobacco while they're not "on the clock."

Bill 180 would seek to repeal that law, and has been referred to the Senate Committee on Labor, Commerce and Industry.

South Carolina, which is possibly the most pro-tobacco state in the Union, is not expected to pass the bill.

## Ireland Ratifies Law That Bans Smoking In Cars With A Child Present

IRELAND- Smoking in any vehicle with a child under the age of 18 present will net you a fine of €3,000 (about $4,000 USD).

The controversial law faced stiff opposition due to a few technicalities, namely, "proving" that the adult actually smoked tobacco within the vehicle. The law gave police the right to impose the fine based solely on visual evidence. Most legislators that voted against the bill did so mainly because of this broad authority given to law enforcement.

As it stands, if a policeman *believes* that he saw a cigarette or tobacco product in use within the vehicle, the person can be convicted, even if no tobacco products are found on his person or within the vehicle.

## Dominican Family Enters The Twentieth Century, Confused by Strange Customs

**AP-** A Canadian airline says it had to divert a plane to Bermuda because a family was openly smoking in their seats.

A spokesman for Sunwing Vacations says the plane bound for the Dominican Republic from Halifax made an emergency landing at L.F. Wade International Airport on Friday night because a mother, father and son refused to butt out.

Daryl McWilliams says the family became verbally abusive and refused to tell the crew where they had stashed their cigarette butts.

The Bermuda Police Service says a 54-year-old man, a 52-year-old woman and a 22-year-old man were arrested after the plane landed and they were later released on bail.

McWilliams says the plane had to be searched and the cigarette butts were eventually located. He says the plane's 180 passengers and crew stayed in a hotel overnight and the aircraft resumed its journey on Saturday afternoon.

## Australians "Stick It To" Plain Label Law

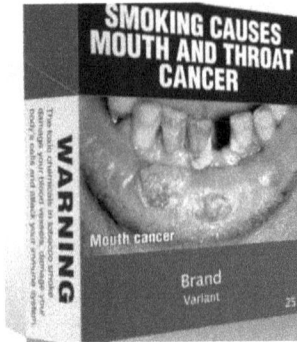

Australia's government probably didn't expect tobacco consumers to find away around their plain packaging law that makes all cigarette packages uniformly ugly.

The law makes each cigarette pack carry a disgusting cancer pic on its front and back, giant warning labels on each side, and the brand's name printed on a small olive drab label near the bottom of the pack.

While discussing the nanny state law over a pint one night, two Yatala mates who run their own print shop, Anthony Do Rozario and Joel Whittaker, came up with a simple, but brilliant idea. "Let's make adhesive stickers that perfectly fit the cigarette pack, so smokers won't have to see a black lung every time they light up," they said.

The duo introduced a series of stickers that portray everything from the Australian flag to nearly-nude models under the brand name "Box Wrap." The stickers easily cover the entire cigarette pack, and it were an immediate hit with smokers. Box Wrap first began selling the stickers online, but retailer orders hit the roof almost from the get-go. De Rozario explained that "We didn't expect the retail demand. Once we got on the national news, the emails started flooding in from national retailers." Now it's hard to find a convenience store or tobacco outlet that doesn't carry Box Wrap stickers.

One such tobacconist explained the appeal of Box Wraps. "They're very inexpensive [about .17 USD] and almost all smokers buy them. They'll buy a pack of cigarettes and a sticker to go along with it, and immediately discard the plastic wrap on the packet and affix the sticker to the box. Nobody likes the new [cigarette pack] designs, so they want to cover them up as quickly as possible."

No word yet on when the Aussie government intends to ban the sale of stickers.

## Canadian Customs Seize 30,000 Pounds of Tobacco

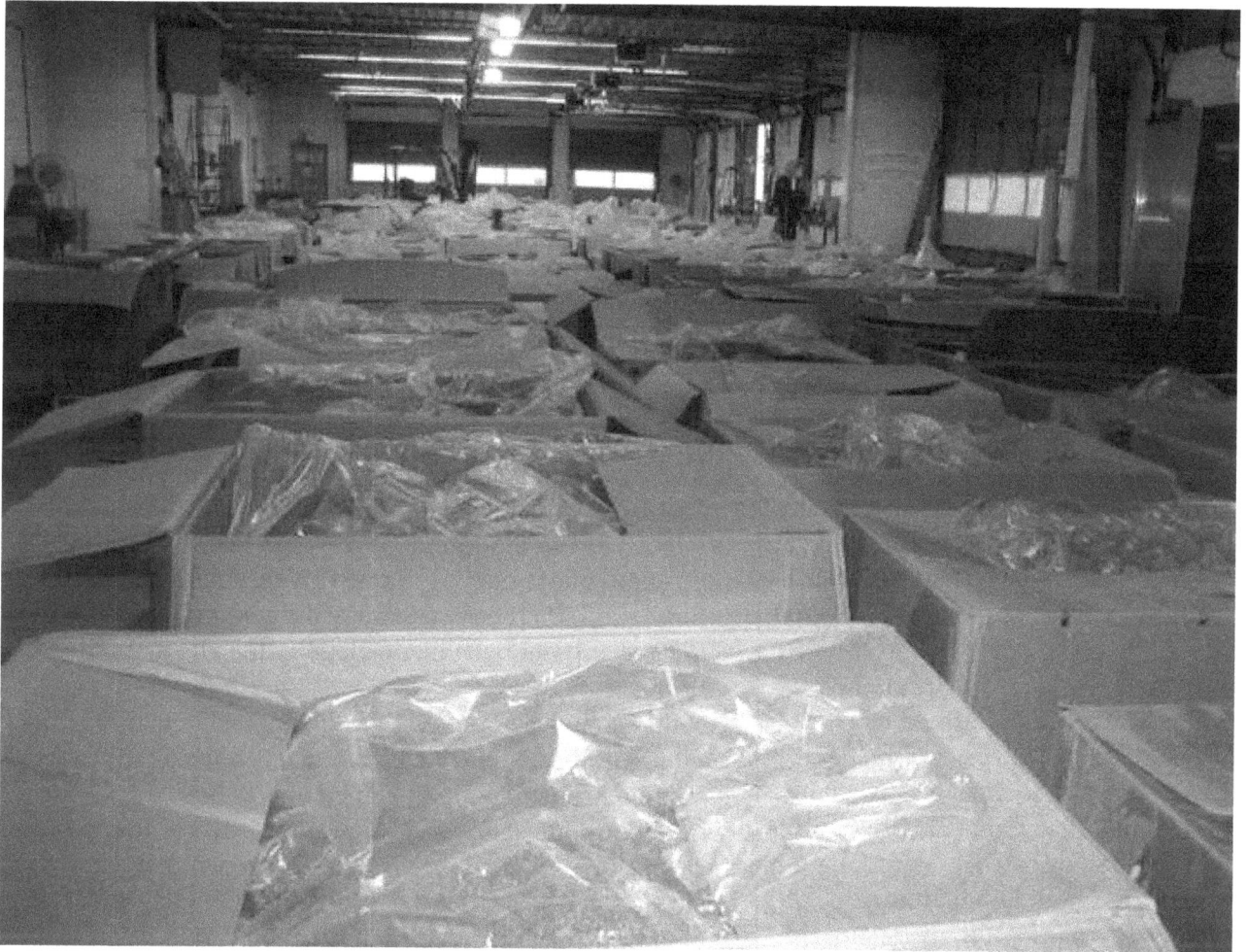

**Ontario, January 10th-** A commercial truck crossing the border into Canada from Detroit was detained and inspected Thursday and was found to contain 30,000 pounds of grade-A Virginia burley (pictured above).

The unnamed driver claimed that he was hauling beans and rice, but Canuck officials at the border were of course suspicious, mainly because Canadians don't eat beans and/or rice. When Customs Agents began inspecting the cargo, they were shocked to find the golden brown contraband.

The "street value" of the tobacco is worth almost two million Canadian dollars. (The same amount would fetch less than $35,000 in the United States). "The CBSA takes its border-protection responsibilities very seriously, and our officers work diligently to prevent smuggling across our borders," Rick Comerford, regional director general for the agency's southern Ontario region, said in a press release.

"This seizure clearly demonstrates that our officers are vigilant when it comes to ensuring our border is not used for illegal activities. This includes prosecuting those who contravene the Customs Act," he went on.

We at the Ephemeris wish to thank those "vigilant" officers for keeping this dangerous junk out of the hands of Canadian children.

## Big Fat Liar Loses Arizona Senate Race To Another Big Fat Liar

*Senator Jeff Flake (left) and former Surgeon General Dr. Richard Carmona*

Former Surgeon General (under George W. Bush) Richard Carmona (Democrat) lost the heavily contested Arizona senate seat to Jeff Flake (Republican).

You may recall Carmona, while serving as Surgeon General, famously lying to the world when he proclaimed that "smokeless tobacco is 100% as dangerous as smoking, therefore should be treated like cigarettes," calling for an exhaustive legislative action that would later pass as part of the Kennedy-Waxman act.

Flake is no slouch in the truth-stretching department either. While changing positions on nearly everything he's campaigned for or against at one time, he at least had the decency to admit that "I lied. I don't know what else to say," when questioned as to why he broke his own campaign trail term-limit pledge.

We're still waiting for Carmona's apology.

## WHOluminatti: UN Holds Secret Sessions to Determine the Fate of the Worldwide Tobacco Trade

SEOUL South Korea- The World Health Organization, the United Nations' public health policy arm, has banned the press and the public from current and future tobacco talks this past November.

The semi-regular Convention on Tobacco Control Policy (COP, for short) has met traditionally to discuss worldwide tobacco control initiatives, such as the EU snus ban and E-Cigarette taxation and prohibition.

CAN #5, a two-day event held in Seoul, was supposedly held "to ratify an agreement to fight smuggled and pirated tobacco products across the globe." For some reason, INTERPOL, the agency most likely to be involved with these proposed efforts, was barred from attending the conferences for reasons that have still not been made clear by the UN or WHO.

But the second, and biggest "WTF" moment occurred on the second day, when talks suddenly shifted towards a comprehensive plan for all UN nations to raise tobacco taxes worldwide. As reported by Newsmax's Drew Johnson, "as the session began, the session's chairwoman expressed concern that there was a "large presence" of tobacco growers and industry representatives in the public gallery."

The conversation immediately stopped and the public was quickly escorted from the gallery, including the representatives of the tobacco industry. Amid mutterings of "unfairness" and "secret agendas," all members of the international press were also ejected from the proceedings.

What happened next is unclear (since there is no public record of the proceedings) but the WHO did announce that it gave the EU its "Dirty Ashtray Award" for not having high enough tobacco taxes.

If you live in a country that belongs to the UN, then your tax dollars are paying for these closed door sessions, which are supposed to be open to the public. It's high time that we (literally) get to see what we're paying for.

## Strange Bedfellows: Why Is Liggett & Myers Giving Henry Waxman Hundreds of Thousands of Dollars?

*"What, me crooked?" Waxman's campaign manager Lindsay Bubar claims she "didn't know [Liggett] contributed until I received this inquiry and was only aware there was an ad after it was on the radio."*

We all know why Phillip Morris supported the PACT Act and the Kennedy/Waxman FDA bill. The laws, particularly the Kennedy/Waxman act, virtually guaranteed Phillip Morris a foothold over its competition from other tobacco manufacturers (leaving it to be dubbed the "Marlboro Preservation Act" by critics of the bill) by reducing their efforts to market safer alternatives to smoking.

But why has Waxman's personal super PAC, the "Committee for an Effective and Trusted Congressman," received hundreds of thousands of dollars from Liggett Vector for the last decade? Why would the nation's biggest anti-tobacco politician accept money from one of the world's largest tobacco manufacturers? In September alone, Waxman's PAC received $33,000 from Liggett & Myers.

We've noticed that since L&M began to aggressively pump Waxman's wallet full of money last year, all of the talk about the FDA banning menthol from cigarettes (which would effectively bankrupt Liggett & Myers, makers of Newport cigarettes) has virtually disappeared.

Coincidence? Suuuuuuuuurrree.

## Actor Richard Briers Dies, Aged 79

LONDON- Famed British Actor Richard Briers passed away from complications following Emphysema on the 18th of February. He had just turned 79 in January.

A staple of English film and television since the 1960's, Briers is perhaps best known by American audiences for his roles in several Kenneth Branagh films such as *Much Ado About Nothing*, *Hamlet*, and *Mary Shelly's Frankenstein*. He's also appeared in various episodes of *Doctor Who* and did voice work for the *Bob the Builder* animated series.

In an interview with the Associated Press last year, Briers claims that he must have smoked "at least a half a million cigarettes in my career." He stopped smoking about ten years ago, switching to nasal snuff to help curb his cravings. "But it was too late, the ciggies got me. I stopped 10 years ago, but too late," he told the *Daily Mail* newspaper last month. "It's totally my fault. So, I get very breathless, which is a pain in the backside."

He was named an Officer in the Order of the British Empire in 1989 shortly after completing a nearly 30 year stage run in Hamlet. He was well known for his straightforward, in-your-face delivery that separated him from other Shakespearean actors. "I once saw a chap take two minutes to build up to a soliloquy, walking around in circles to build up anticipation. I said, 'What a lark!' and so I made it a point to deliver my lines as quickly as possible. I think I may not have been the best Hamlet of my generation but I was certainly the fastest. On the opening night I took 24 minutes off the running time, and I think it must have been the only 'Hamlet' in recent times where people were able to get out to the pub afterwards for a drink," he said.

Briers is survived by his wife of 57 years and two daughters.

# New Items
## Stuff That's Come Out Since Last Issue

- **Skoal Ready Cut (Pre-portioned cubes):** Mint, Wintergreen, Straight (USST)
- **Red Man Magenta Oral Snuff** (Not officially released yet) (SM)
- **Grov Stark Original** (SM)
- **Kronan Stark White Portion** (SM)
- **6 Photo: Super Chetak Moist**
- **Absolut Menthol (non-tobacco snus)**
- **General White Mint Long** (SM)
- **Kaliber Special White** (SM)
- **FUBAR: SNAFU**
- **FUBAR: SNAFU Menthol**
- **FUBAR: FUGAZI Black Joe**
- **FUBAR: FUGAZI Menthol**
- **De Kralingse: Mississippi**
- **De Kralingse: Limburgertabak**
- **Poschl Grado**
- **Sir Walter Scott: Mull of Oa**
- **41 Photo: White Elephant**
- **6 Photo: Motia**
- **7 Photo: Swami**
- **7 Photo: Bijli Naswar**
- **Bernard: Steife Prise**
- **Bernard: Weinachtspris**
- **Paul Gotard: Gooseberry Snuff bottle**
- **Paul Gotard: Juniper Snuff bottle**
- **Paul Gotard: Pear Snuff bottle**
- **Paul Gotard: Rhubarb Snuff bottle**
- **Stok: Rosa Li, J. Rummy, Strawberry, Peach**
- **Xuefu**
- **Xuefu Mint**
- **Ink Black Rock** (AG)
- **Ink Red Devil** (AG)
- **Kapten 24 White** and **Original** Portions (AG)
- **Old Ving 99** (Coffee) (GN)
- **Old Ving Melon** (GN)
- **Supporter Snus (North Europe Division)**- 16 Varieties (All the same flavor as Blagul)
- **Nord 66 White** and **Regular** (Skruf)
- **Nord 66 Nordic Breeze** (Skruf)
- **Oden's Extra** and **Extreme** Lakrits (GN)
- **Oden's Extreme Cold Ultra Strong** (GN)
- **Thunder Ultra Original** (v2)
- **Thunder White Wintergreen** (v2)
- **Lab Series 12** Fresh Mint (SM)
- **Catch White Spearmint Long** (SM)
- **Nick and Johnny Green Spyke Extra Strong Cactus Snus** (SM)
- **Oden's 69 Extreme Dry White Portions** (GN)
- **Skruf Slim Cranberry** and **Strong White Portions** (Skruf)
- **Catch Collection** Madison Avenue Edition (SM)
- **General White** Tailored Fit (SM)
- **General Lakrits** (SM)
- **Camel Wintergreen** and **Straight** Oral Snuffs (RJR)
- **Abraxas Cafe 11**
- **Abraxas FireDrac**
- **Cerise** (Special Edition) (Abraxas)
- **Sam Gawith** 2013 LTD (SG)
- **Viceroy Snus Packets** (Regular, Mint, Wintergreen (RJR)
- **Revel Dissolvables** (Regular, Wintergreen) (RJR)

# Letters

## THE GREATEST LETTER IN THE HISTORY OF ALL LETTERS

Snuff Takers Ephemeris is the WORST magazine ever sold! And so are all the other snuff magazines. How could you people worship such trash! I am the father of an 11 year old snuff freak. And as head of the house, I finally put my foot down and made a rule that I should have made years ago. NO SNUFF MOVIES, MAGAZINES, OR SUCH GARBAGE IN THE HOUSE AT ANYTIME!

I am appalled with the trash my son started bringing into this house! Why does he pay money for something he can get at the dump for free? The world doesn't need your junk- it's bad enough as it is. Unfortunately, Eric never misses an issue. He tells me how much they cost, but to me it's just bird cage liner. When he gets a new issue, I want to tear out what hair I have left! And to top it off, his room is covered with snuff posters, models, books and pictures! He may as well sleep under the house!

Anyone who has anything to do with snuff must be mentally deranged! Don't give me your psychology crap! What about all these murders happening today? What do you think is the cause of it? That's right- SNUFF! What do you see in it? Snuff is not an art form. It's just crap! Your rag is just a cheap scheme to make a dollar. Don't say it's good for children! What made me put my foot down was Eric's attitude towards his brother, Alan. He laid out all of your stupid magazines to show his brother. Well, Alan walked into his room, and Eric took one of the magazines and held it up to Alan's face, and began to growl! Poor Alan ran to his room, screaming and sobbing.

That was the last straw! For years I put up with his snuff trash, but I ended it all that day! I recalled an article from one of your rags about a guy burning up all his back issues of STE. What a good idea! So I took all of his snuff posters, books, models, and best of all his shitty bunch of STE, threw em' in the fireplace, and began the sacred burning! What a crybaby he was!

I also took away his weekly allowance. Whenever I see a snuff article in his room or in his hand, I quickly confiscate it for burning. I know he hates me, but I know what I'm doing is for the best. Someday he'll thank me for this. I have forbidden him to see any snuff movies, but YOU warped his mind so much he won't listen to Me. I know what's good for him, and the sooner he appreciates the Bach, Chopin and opera music I brought him, and starts reading Shakespeare and Hemingway and the Bible, the sooner he get's his allowance back.

I also make him read National Geographic and Readers Digest, good magazines, not like yours. So, I'm throwing out all his rock and roll-snuff trash, and giving him a decent haircut. You're the cause of this and I'm glad I'm finally taking action. I hope you print this letter, maybe it'll finally change the minds of all the sicko parents who read your cheap, good for nothing rag, but you won't- because you'll get other letters agreeing with me.

If I had my way, I would have you and all of your followers executed, and your junky snuff museum and publishing company burned up, along with all the snuff movies. I hope your company goes bankrupt. What kind of editor are you, clogging every page of your worthless rag begging for handouts for your worthless snuff magazine? Why don't you go out on the streets of Fayetteville? Maybe you'll get even more money. I hope My son Eric never lays eyes on you, you greedy old bastard! How could you even try to sell your book to kids? There's naked pictures and tobacco everywhere, and not the normal kind like cigarettes, but the kind you snort like cocaine or keep in your mouth like pills. You must all be drug addicts or something. It wouldn't surprise me considering that you all are degenerates and devil worshippers.

I'll bet you 5,000 dollars that you know I'm right and you're wrong. I don't care what you, Eric or any of your stupid worshippers think. I know I'm right. I'm leaving my address out, because I don't want to be bombarded by any of your bombastic imbecile followers. I don't have time to waste on your snuff crap. I'll bet you another 5,000 dollars you won't print this letter because deep down you know you have mental problems, and you know I'm right.

Scott Rogers,
Bunnlevel, N.C.

*Mr. Rogers, you almost had yourself $5,000 dollars. See, you were right when you bet us that we were wrong and you were right and that we had mental problems, but then you bet us another $5,000 that we wouldn't print the letter. So it's a wash.*

Guys,

Who was the girl in the bathtub in the last issue?

David

*Good question. Maybe she'll get in touch with us so we can give her proper credit, just like the other 15 models we hired that don't seem to want to be affiliated with us. They probably have the same opinion of us that Scott Rogers does, so what's a*

*bunch of poor degenerates to do? Seriously girls, write me back so we can give you proper credit.*

Hi gang,

I realize I'm a bit belated in doing so, but I wanted to thank you for my previous order of STE Vol. VI. When it arrived, I was pleasantly surprised to find that I received a numbered, signed, certified first-day printing of the magazine - very cool!

I also really enjoy the newer, larger format of STE, and am happy to see that you all keep working hard to continue publishing - and continue improving - this one-of-a-kind magazine.

Again, thank you very much, and keep up the awesome work!

Jeremy Duettra

*We appreciate the feedback Jeremy! We strive hard to put out the best magazine we can every month. Sometimes it happens, sometimes it doesn't. But I think Volume VI was indeed one of our high points. Thanks for writing and we hope you stick around for a long time.*

Sirs/Madams/Etc,

I was highly disappointed with the new direction the magazine took when you went to the large format. It costs more to ship, it's in black and white, and above all it's expensive. It seems like the "magic", if you will, that you captured with #s 1-4 is all but gone, save for a few spots here and there. I am having a hard time justifying the purchase anymore.

John Richardson

*John, we're sorry to hear that you aren't digging the new issues. I agree that the first couple of issues were our best, and then we hit a small lull, and then we picked up steam with our most recent issues. We're just now entering our third year of publication and we've learned a lot along the way.*

*We made many mistakes at first, and although I miss the full color of the digest-sized early issues, there's absolutely no comparison to the print quality of our new run. We're producing the magazine that we intended to put out from the very beginning, but were too naive and cash-strapped to accomplish. We hope you stick around, and thank you for your honest criticism.*

Hey,

I was wondering why not you all do an article about all the hot little girlies on youtube making their own dip videos? There's a bunch of them out there, and I can give you a list of them if y'all need it.

Chris,
Virginia

*Well Chris, we like gal's dipping snuff just as much as the next guy. But I've really yet to see a good "girl doing dip" vid on youtube. It's just basically 16 year olds going "Hey y'all, I got this here Griz Green and I'm finna tear it up" while some really obnoxious rap song or nerve-grating country tune is playing in the background.*

*Maybe when the girls turn 18 and learn to formulate complete sentences, we'll re-evaluate our stance on female dip vids. BTW, everybody reading this magazine needs to check out Redneck Whooty's videos. She's the queen of all youtube chick dippers. For realz.*

Despite what was said in your magazine, Bela Lugosi was a communist through and through.

Adam

*No, he wasn't. Thanks for writing though.*

What was it like interviewing Christopher Lee?

Chris

*Chris wants to know what it was like to interview Chris. Well Chris, in one word, it was kind of awkward. Chris Lee is a living legend, and though he is a cranky old man when people ask him the same tired questions (about vampires, horror, etc) he becomes very warm and open when you talk to him about something that actually interests him.*

*We talked at a convention, not the greatest place to conduct interviews, granted, but he perked right up when I started talking about Peter Cushing and snuff. I also brought him some familial charts that he took home with him (turns out we're 12th cousins) and he thanked me greatly. A gentleman through and through. Then some fat bastard ran up behind me and basically shoved me out of the way and said "So what was it like working with Johnny Depp?" I could see his Mr. Lee's eyes roll as he repeated the same anecdote that he had told so many times that day. But he trooped along, never missing a beat.*

*So if you're reading this Chris, hello from your cousin in the US, and we hope you've been enjoying the magazine.*

Hey Dude, I really dug the pics of the girls, do you think you could put some different types of pics in your next mag? You know, pics like in the old body-building mags, like Steve Reeves or other dudes. Thanks,

Your pal,
D. Quinn, ESQ.
Dunn NC

*You mean like this?*

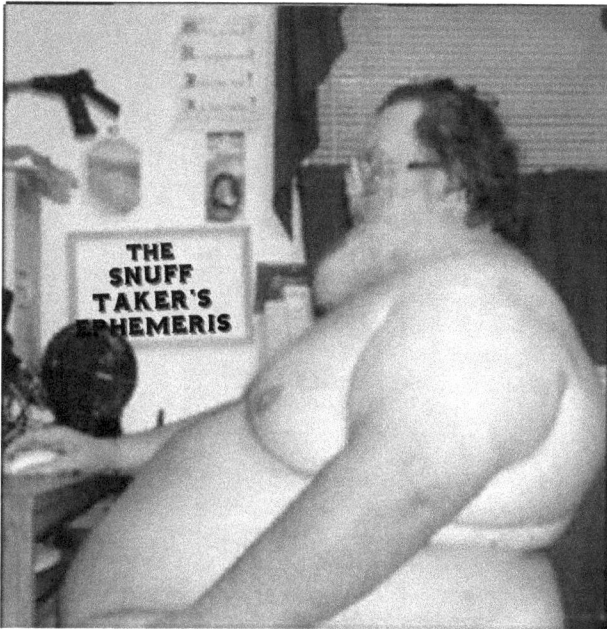

Was that really you guys at the White House? [Last Issue]. Who was that faggot wearing a neckerchief?

"Don Vito"

*That little faggot with the earring and the makeup? (Yeah buddy, that's his own hair!)*

*Seriously though, we're still not sure of his identity. He just wandered up to the podium while we were taking pictures. We heard that he has his own jet airplane and is a millionaire, for what it's worth.*

## Letter of the Month

Let me sum up how I feel in just 23 words: It's the best magazines on the stands, both internet and bookstore, and I hope it outlives all of us reading this right now.

Thank you for your magazine,
Ahmed Briehat
Chicago, IL

*Thank you Ahmed, you old brown-noser. Look for a year's subscription heading your way with Volume Nine.*

Why can't you guys keep a straight schedule? You are supposed to be quarterly but you come out like two or three times a year.

Chris.

*Well Chris (lots of Chrises this issue for some reason), aside from our first issue (which came out late that first year), we've always put out four issues per annum. Last year we put out six, if you count the "Night Before Christmas" book. So even if we come out in odd intervals, we've ALWAYS been a quarterly and plan to keep it that way.*

*Another good answer to your question is that we spend way too much time reading letters. Nevertheless, bring them on:*

Letters@STEphemeris

STE
PO Box 287
Spring Lake, NC
28390 USA

*See you in, uh, later this year sometime...*

WARNING: This product can cause mouth cancer.

# Blah Blah Blah

*Publisher's note:* First off, I wish to say "I'm sorry" for two things in this issue (and last): we've lost our ability to do full bleed illustrations. (For those not in the industry, it means that the image literally extends off the edge of the page.) Our book has now been neutered into a standardized "four white margins" because according to our printer, "It's too difficult [to publish the Ephemeris] with the way you lay out your graphics, especially in greyscale." Sorry for thinking that a printing press would be able to work with the most basic of presentations, but then again these are American printers we're talking about, so maybe this is their way of saying "go to China! We don't need your business!" (As always, our digital edition will remain full color/full bleed.)

Second off, I want to sincerely apologize for featuring not just one, but two "interviews" with me in the same edition. I'm not an egomaniac, but the radio interview has been sitting around since last issue and we ran out of room for it. The second, an IRC chat that I did earlier last month, is about an issue that I've been wanting to address for a while now: our cover price.

So here is the IRC chat in its entirety, unedited. I've condescendingly named the other guy "whiner guy" because that's what I've determined him to be. (I named myself "Me" for simplification.)

**Whiner Guy:** So here's my only beef with STE. Why so much?

Me: *So much what?*

**WG:** Expensive

Me: *What, the cover price?*

**WG:** Yup

**WG:** That's like twice as much as other magazines

Me: *What magazines are you talking about specifically?*

**[2 minute pause]**

**WG:** So I have a TV Guide, a Time and a Peiple and they're all between 3-5 dollards. Your magaizine is twice as much as that.

Me: *Have you ever heard of the difference between "specialty magazine" and "mass media?"*

**WG:** Yeah

Me: *Well, you realize we're a specialty publication right?*

**WG:** Yeah but that's twice as much as what I usually pay for a magazine.

Me: *What specialty magazines do you buy?*

**WG:** I don't know, but I buy like *Gamepro* and *Nintendo Power* for my little brother.

Me: *They're, what, six or seven bucks an issue?*

**WG:** I don't know. I don't have one handy.

Me: *And how many ads do they have?*

**WG:** I don't know, a pretty good bit.

Me: *And I bet you buy them at your local Gamestop, newsstand, Wal-mart or grocery chain?*

**WG:** Yeah.

Me: *Well, there you go. You can buy them anywhere, they've got tons of ads, and there's millions of gamers out there ready to snatch them up. Those aren't exactly "niche" magazines. In fact, with what the different gaming companies pay to advertise in their pages, they could afford to print 50,000 copies and not even bother releasing them; they've already turned a profit. Just from ad revenue.*

WG: So you're saying that if you get more ad money the price could be cheaper?

Me: *Sure, if you want us to run 30 pages of ads for whatever products come to us for marketing. As it stands, we've lost two of our main advertisers when we switched to black and white and these last two issues didn't generate enough ad revenue to even cover the printing cost. We could start running ads for spray-on hair replacement and Sham-wows, but I don't think our core audience would appreciate it. So right now we're not really even breaking even unless we get paying advertisers to step up to the plate and help us out.*

**[Long Pause.]**

WG: All I'm saying is that 10 bucks is out of my budget.

Me: *Actually, it's 11 bucks if you buy it in the store. We knock a buck off to compensate for having to have it shipped for you.*

WG: So it's 15 bucks?

Me: *No, it's 14 bucks. Then add another dollar shipping for two issues. We cap the shipping off at 5.15.*

WG: How much is it on Amazon?

Me: *I don't know. Lots of stores carry it. I imagine it would be 10.99 plus 3.99 shipping per issue. But some stores get quantity discounts depending on how much they order, so you might find stores selling it for the same thing we sell it for on our website. But again, our shipping would be the same for one copy or cheaper if you tbuy on Amazon if you order two or more.*

Me: *If you subscribe, your shipping is free.*

WG: What about sales tax?

Me: *Do you live in NC?*

WG: No, I live in Nebraska.

Me: *Well, then we won't collect sales tax.*

**[Short pause.]**

Me: *Have you even ever ordered anything online?*

WG: No, not really much. I try to buy it locally

Me: *Have you got a bookstore in your town?*

WG: I think maybe

Me: *You know they can order the book for you and you can go pick it up, right?*

WG: Yeah, but it's still too high for my blood.

Me: *What about the digital editions? They're 4.99. That's cheaper than your brother's Gamepro and Nintendo Powers.*

WG: But I've never read a copy, so I don't know if it's worth me paying 5 bux to even read one.

Me: *Oh.*

WG: Yeah, and will it work on my Kindle?

Me: *It's a .pdf. If your Kindle reads .pdf's then yes. If not, no.*

WG: I'm not sure, never tried PDF

Me: *So what do you want from me? You say that 10 dollars is too high for the magazine, so I tell you about our 5 dollar version, and now you want a free sample?*

**[Long Pause]**

Me: *Hello? We have a free newsletter that publishes sample pages and articles from upcoming issues. You can sign up right there on the website. That's as free as we get, because quite frankly, if you can't afford to gamble 5 dollars then I don't know how you can afford to be on the internet.*

**[Long Pause]**

{Whiner Guy has exited the chat.}

**********

I printed this chat not because I'm bitter or angry, it's just a question that comes up frequently and I happened to be able to copy the chatlog here to basically answer dozens of letters that would otherwise clog up our letter page every month.

For the record, the three or four magazines I get every month (*Retrogamer, Fangoria, Scary Monsters* and *Famous Monsters*) all cost about 10 dollars or more per issue. (*I read at least another half dozen periodicals per month, but those are the main four that I pick up without fail, since I have a complete run of each and don't want to "break" the collection up. Chalk it up to OCD*). I guarantee their readership is larger than ours, and the sheer amount of ads they run per copy tells me that they've got a solid ad revenue coming in. Their circulation hovers between 10-25,000 copies per issue. Cut those numbers in half and you have the circulation for the Ephemeris. Yet, we're all grouped together as "niche specialty periodicals" and are expected to be priced the same. We do this, even though it takes money out of our pockets and isn't really fair to us to be expected to compete with these other guys. But we do it because I refuse to price the magazine any higher than it already is.

All of our contributors are volunteers, and if/when we do make a profit it goes directly back into the magazine. I spend 50-60 hours a week writing or publishing, with very little return on my efforts. Please don't be under the impression that every time we sell a copy of the Ephemeris, 10 bucks goes in my pocket and pretty soon I'll have my Rolls Royce paid off. It's not like that at all.

As I said, I'm sorry to have even breached this topic to begin with but we field criticisms like this one so often that I finally felt compelled to say something about it. At least now when someone asks me why the book costs so much, I can say "read my editorial in issue 8, you damned cheapskate" and end the conversation right there.

**********

On the flipside of the coin, we have numerous dedicated readers (God Bless you all) who inquire as to whether there is anything they can do to help boost awareness of our book. Yes, you can. If you see a smokeless tobacco manufacturer (not RJR or Phillip Morris) that isn't advertising in our book, WRITE or CALL them and pester them until they do! Our rates are ultra affordable and when you run an ad with us, we treat you like royalty. (We'll still tell you if your product sucks though.) You can also tune in to our media pages like our blog, facebook and youtube accounts and "like," subscribe or "thumbs up" as much of our stuff as you can. Till next time,

RW Hubbard

Whiny Greedy Capitalist

# Whiskey, Sex and Snus: The Snuffers That Built America

## By RW Hubbard

*We often hear that America was built by visionaries like Vanderbilt and Rockefeller. While it's true that they built great business empires and became some of the wealthiest men in the world, the actual **work** was done by an entirely different class of people. Thousands of laborers (both skilled and unskilled) played a game of "follow the money" in the late 1800's and early 1900's. Mostly immigrants, these men would head to the Pacific Northwest to mine copper and lay tracks for railroads. They would flood Chicago and New York and help erect the giant buildings that still stand today. Or they might go down to Texas and work an oil rig. Eventually, they would end up in Detroit, Michigan where the steady demand for automobiles hasn't ceased since the first Model T rolled off the line.*

*This article focuses on one group in particular: the Scandinavian railroaders who left their homelands to lay tracks in America. Though they helped build up the railroads all over the US, the wages in the Pacific Northwest were the highest, especially in Alaskan territory. The work was so grueling and the weather so cold that the first group to attempt work in that area, the Chinese, dropped their pickaxes and headed back to California in terror. Though the wages in the south were a fraction of what they could have made in the north, the Chinese favored lower pay over unsettled territory, hypothermia, bear attacks, and 24 hour a day sub-zero temperatures.*

*The next group to step in were the Russians, who were hard workers and managed well in the cold, but unskilled at building railroads. For a while, it looked like the great experiment in Northwestern railroading was going to end up being a fiasco that would cost investors millions of dollars and years of wasted time.*

*But then the third group came. These were Norsemen; mainly Swedes and Danes, but also Finns, Norwegians, Dutch and Icelanders. These men were experienced track layers. After a series of wars, droughts and financial catastrophes, the Nordic railroad program screeched to a halt and thousands were left without a job. They knew about the American railroad and how it was in need of workers, and they knew that they faced stiff competition from other immigrant groups in terms of finding work. At the very bottom of the ladder, below the Chinese, below the Blacks, even below the Polish- there stood the Swede, ready to prove himself to his bosses and earn a good living while doing so. The Swede had heard about the Northwest, and how it was so miserable that nobody worked there longer than a week. With pickaxe on his shoulder, the Swede headed toward Washington State to show them how it was done. This is where our article begins.*

It was the golden age of Westward Expansion in the United States. There was a rush for gold up and down the West Coast, on into Alaska. There was only one problem- there was no way to transport it back to civilization. The early Alaskan pioneers needed a good trade route that allowed them to get from any point in Alaska down to Dutch Harbor, which would allow them to sail back to the coast of Washington state (thereby bypassing the dangerous- and expensive- Yukon route.) The pioneers needed ports and shipbuilders, but more importantly, they needed trains and railroads. What good was it to find two tons of gold if you had no way to transport it?

Soon word spread all over that skilled workers were needed in the Alaskan territory. Laborers came from all over the world to lend a hand in the Alaskan boom years. The Dutch and the Norwegians arrived as shipbuilders and fishermen. The Greeks and the Russians came to mine ore and copper. From down south in California, the Irish and the Chinese came to build the railroad. And finally, there came the Swedes, to do a little bit of everything.

Sweden during the latter part of the nineteenth century was not an easy place to live. Drought, famine, wars and plague sent many Swedes away from their homeland, and the majority of those that left went to America. The Swedish were diligent workers, and they had little trouble finding work in the New Country. They carried with them a reputation for hard work and even harder reverie.

The only real route that carried the Swedes into the new world was the Gothenburg-Chicago route on the British & Wilson Line. The route ran all the way from Göteborg, Sweden to Seattle, Washington. If you were to trace this route on a map today, you would see the towns and settlements that sprang up virtually overnight with a Swedish population. Many stayed where they first set foot on American soil, in and around Holgate, New Jersey (as dock workers) and the town of Helmetta (as factory workers).

Those that went a little bit further on would find the farms of Pennsylvania a welcome reminder of their past lives. When Pennsylvania became overrun with Swedes, it became necessary for later immigrants to travel along farther down the route in order to find work. South Michigan, Northern Ohio and Indiana all had sizable Swedish populations, with most of them working in mills and factories. But for most Swedes, up until the twentieth century, Chicago, Illinois was the end of the line. With its endless array of factories, affordable housing, and no shortage of work, Chicago was heaven for most Swedes.

It was said that the Swedes loved only three things: whiskey, sex and snus. Chicago had all three. Most of it was centered on the south end of Washington Street- an area known as Snoose Boulevard (not to be confused with Snoose Junction in Minnesota). The "main drag" was an all night party spot. "You had a lot of bars, a lot of prostitutes, and a lot of snus," claims Nina Clark, historian at the American-Swedish Institute. TOO much for more conservative Swedes, who ended up moving farther down the line. Most found work in the farms of Wisconsin, and the mines of Minnesota and the Dakotas.

The Greyhound Bus Lines, for example, had its roots in Hibbing, Minnesota (birthplace of Bob Dylan.) The Wickman-Anderson Bus Lines, an early progenitor of Greyhound, got its start by hauling Swedish miners all over the Twin Cities area. This was called the "Snus Line", and to get the driver to stop and pick you up, it was said that you had to wave a can of snus

# Direkte till Amerika

med

**Anchor-Liniens Transatlantiska Ångbåts-Bolag**

som befordrar Emigranter

med egna

för Emigrantbefordring afsedda

1:sta klassens ångare

## "Scandinavia" & "Scotia"

från Göteborg hvarje Tisdag.

Tolkar medfölja från Göteborg ända till Chicago

Göteborg år 1870.

**JOHN MILLAR,**

Anchor-Liniens General-Agent för Sverige.

*Left:* "Direct to America: Carrying Emigrants from Göteborg to Chicago." *Handbill, ca. 1830.*

*So many Swedes immigrated to the US during this period that most shiplines offered exclusive travel packages. A ship would take the passenger from Gothenburg to New Jersey, where a train would take the rider to Chicago. Unfortunately, some of these travel packages were scams, and the Swede would find himself stranded in New York or New Jersey without a train ticket to carry them the rest of the way. These carriers were called "drop runners," as they would literally drop their passengers off and sail away as quickly as possible.*

*Above: The Swedish Emigration lasted well into the 20th century. Above is a 1905 postcard, "Farewell to Home," depicting Gothenburg residents leaving Sweden for Great Britain and the US.*

his direction and hand it over as bus fare!

Still other Swedes were attracted to the high-paying lumber industry that dominated the Pacific Northwest. This was known as the "Last Leg" of the Gothenburg-Chicago route, and only the hardiest, most determined Swedes were willing to make it that far into an already months-long journey. It's no surprise that these men were willing to make their living as lumberjacks; it was said that if you survived the British & Wilson Line, you could survive anything.

Many of these loggers were from Northern Sweden, and most were familiar with building railroads. When the call came out from Alaska, the Swedes showed up immediately, tools in hand, ready to work.

Michael J. "Jack" Heney commenced work on the Copper River and Northwestern Railway, the first railroad into Alaskan Yukon territory. Many questioned his tenacity, as they clearly viewed his plan as a fools errand. Ever confident, Heney is famously quoted as saying "Give me enough snus and dynamite and I can build you a road to Hell!" Heney used Swedish labor exclusively, as he felt that "they all work until quitting time. Then they drink too much, get into fights, sleep it off, and are ready to commence again at daybreak."

With the success of Heney's venture, others came following suit to try their hand at railroading. Tracks were built adjacent to mining camps, fish camps and trading posts. Some labor groups floated between trades effortlessly, following the almighty dollar. This led to an often disparate living environment composed of different cultures and ethnicities all working and cohabitating in the same camp. One author remarked on the surreal sights and sounds of the typical Alaskan railroad camp of the day: "[There was a] roaring dance hall. Snus and whiskey. Accordions and fiddles. Songs and stories. German Polkas, Swedish Hambos [a type of folk dance] and Scottish Jigs..."

In working together, these diverse groups shared with each other different customs and habits indigenous to their culture. Among the stories and songs that they traded, they also swapped different methods for taking tobacco. The Scandinavians had been using moist snuff for over a century, and the snus that they used was unique among the still prevalent dry snuffs favored by the Chinese and Irish.

The Swedes often hurled thinly veiled insults at their Scottish and Irish workmates based on their snuff habits. Dry "Scotch" snuff was viewed as feminine by the Scandinavians (as was the practice of taking it nasally), and a common phrase heard throughout the day was "stick around us [Scandinavians] long enough, and we'll teach you how to take snuff like a man!"

Every major trading post dotting the Alaskan wilderness had ample supplies of imported snus. If the Swedes ever ran out of moist snuff, they had a formula for "fixing" nasal snuff. They would empty half a can of dry snuff into another empty container, and then fill both containers to the top with tightly packed ice. The snuff tins would then be strapped securely to a jackhammer which violently mixed the two ingredients together, resulting in a strange pastiche of something approximating Swedish snus. This got a chuckle out of the Irish, who would say things like "Not even a Scotchman is skinflint enough to dilute their snuff in such a manner!"

"Give me enough snus and whiskey, and I'll build you a railroad to hell!" Jack Heney (right) and his men (below.)

# "A Land of Brutal Hostility": The Swedish Government Reacts Negatively Towards the Swedish Emigration

With a country on the brink of socioeconomic destruction, the Swedish monarchy took great strides to prevent the loss of its peasant workforce, who were heading to America in droves. Propaganda flooded the working class streets. One popular tract even went so far as to call potential Emigrants traitors to Sweden: "No workers are more lazy, immoral and indifferent than those who emigrate to other places."

The clergy decried the mass exodus as well. They described America as a barren land full of wild natives and deplorable living conditions. Americans were described as heathen heretics that followed a protestant, and liberal (thus, wrong) ideology.

Per Svenssons nybygge i Amerika: 1. Sådant han drömde sig det.    Per Svenssons nybygge i Amerika. 2. Sådant det i verkligheten blef.

Despite the overwhelmingly positive view of America that was gleaned by letters and postcards from immigrated friends and family members, one Swede who made the American journey painted a very negative image of the country. Per Svensson's "The Real America," above, contrasts the idyllic American image (left) with the reality Svensson experienced in the wilderness of America. Venomous snakes, mountain lions, and murderous Indians did little to deter the Swedish peasantry from making the North American trip.

The Chinese viewed oral snuff use with a sort of repulsed fascination. Many Chinese considered it almost a sacrilege to keep snuff in the mouth for enjoyment; in their culture, snuff was thought to possess magical qualities. The only time it was to be used in the mouth was as a cure for a toothache.

Along with the aforementioned nationalities, there was also a great many Greek and Russian workers that migrated to the railroads. They preferred smoking tobacco, with cigarettes being the most popular method of combustion. Cigarette butts were saved and reused in the evening, where they were packed into the after-dinner pipe. Only the Dutch seemed to share their fondness for smoking, and they would often trade tobacco together. One Dutch fisherman commented on the peculiar way that Russians smoked their cigarettes: "With my own eyes, I swear [I witnessed] a [cigarette smoker] draw the breath deep into his lungs and hold it there. He would speak something in his native tongue, exchange a laugh with his friends, and then blow the pungent smoke back out with a great heave. The [Russians] seem to get intoxicated by the smoke fumes, in a way that we [Dutch] don't tarry." Clearly, inhaling smoke was still a relatively new idea in most cultures at that time.

Though they shared a common heritage, many of the Scandinavians distanced themselves from different Norse groups. Workers from Denmark, Norway, Sweden, Finland, and Iceland often clashed among themselves over past squabbles that were carried over from the "old country". Denmark, Norway and Sweden had been at war with each other off and on for the last century, and there was a lot of animosity between the three, especially between Sweden and Denmark.

Danish workers found it especially ironic that the Swedes loved Copenhagen snuff, a brand that they viewed as a poor substitute for genuine snus. A popular rhyme among the Danes of the time not only painted the Swedes as cowards, but commented on the perceived inferiority of Copenhagen snuff:

*"Ten thousand Swedes*
*Ran through the weeds*
*Chased by one Norwegian.*
*The chaff from the weeds*
*Made snus for the Swedes*
*And they called it Copenhagen!"*

One group that did share the Scandinavian's love for moist snuff was the Polish. The Poles had been making moist snuff for almost a century; they were probably the first culture outside of the Norse to make snuff in that manner. Immigrants from West Poland still favored dry nasal snuff, a tradition that probably had much to do with their shared border with Germany. The people in North Poland (and to a lesser extent, East Poland) shared a very close trade relationship with Sweden, which meant that "Polish" snuff was eventually regarded as a very close relative of Swedish snus.

STE

Make sure to pick up the next edition of The Snuff Taker's Ephemeris for the second, and final, part of this article in which we take a closer look at the men who actually worked the railroads.

# THE DEVIL'S SNUFF

### Exploring the origins and use of the infamous powder

### by
### RW Hubbard & Jim Walter

The morning of October 15th, 1961 started out normally for Rupert Grant. Grant, better known to the music world as Lord Invader, was a Calypso singer best known for penning the Andrews Sisters' 1946 hit *Rum and Coca Cola.* After boiling some coffee on his stove, he walked out on to the steps of his Brooklyn apartment to retrieve the morning paper. As he bent down to pick it up, he clutched at his heart and collapsed. A neighbor called for an ambulance and Grant was taken to the Brooklyn Hospital on Dekalb Avenue, where he died later that evening of complications following a heart attack. He was 47.

His death came as a shock to the folk music community in New York. Grant was thought to be in perfect health and the stories began to run rampant. Rumors circulated that Grant was the victim of a voodoo hex placed on him by a jealous Calypso singer.

Grant's best friend and fellow Calypsonian Cecil Anderson, who went under the stage name "The Duke of Iron," claimed

Lord Invader, ca. 1945

not only to know the identity of the person who allegedly placed the hex, but to know the method by which Grant was killed. Until his death in 1968, the Duke of Iron stated numerous times that someone had sprinkled Devil's Snuff into Grant's coffee grains, poisoning him.

**\*\*\*\*\*\*\*\*\*\***

Devil's Snuff, which has been used by native peoples for thousands of years, is a widely misidentified and usually overlooked fungal seed that grows native to the state of North Carolina and the continent of Northwestern Africa. There are actually two genus of mushrooms which are commonly referred to as "The Devil's Snuffbox": *Lycoperdon perlatum,* a non-poisonous, edible "puffball" mushroom that grows worldwide, and the more elusive (and poisonous) *Scleroderma geaster,* also known as the "Dead Man's Hand," which is used regularly in voodoo/hoodoo rituals for its supposed magical properties. This is the plant that was rumored to have killed Lord Invader. For purpose of clarity, whenever the terms "Devil's Snuffbox" or "Devil's Snuff" is used in this article, it is in reference to the poisonous *geaster* of North America and West Africa.

Comparing the two side by side reveals why the edible Perlatum (left) and the deadly Gleaster (right) are often confused for one another.

They both start off as "puffball" mushrooms (left) and eventually blossom forth in a star pattern (right) yielding a batch of tiny black seeds. Hence, the plant itself is called "The Devil's Snuffbox" while the seeds are known as "The Devil's Snuff."

Devil's Snuff was discovered by the early Native Americans approximately 15,000 years ago and soon took on a minor role in ceremonial rituals. Using the right quantity of seeds brought forth hallucinations, while using too much brought forth death. This helped give *gleaster* a sinister reputation among the native tribes along the east coast, where it once grew as far north as New York. There are several theories as to why it basically died out in all areas outside of the Piedmont region, but the most accepted idea is due to the precise blends of nutrients found in the soil of the Carolinas.

The same phenomenon can be found in modern day Northwestern Africa, which was once linked to North Carolina before the great continental dispersal. The soil of North Africa is very similar to North American Piedmont, which is probably why *gleaster* can still be found growing around the coastal plains and wetlands there. It should be mentioned that the lookalike *perlatum* was used by tribes who were either unaware that it was a different mushroom, or considered it a worthy substitute for *gleaster*. These were the tribes in North America that lived from Georgia to Florida and west of the Appalachians. African tribes that lived apart from the west coast also took to using *perlatum* in place of *gleaster*.

Right:

This globe shows the present day continents before they were split apart during the Great Division.

Devils's Snuff grew within the area marked by the dotted lines, with its heaviest concentration being within the black dot, which represents the areas of present day North Carolina/Virginia and Mauritania of Northwest Africa.

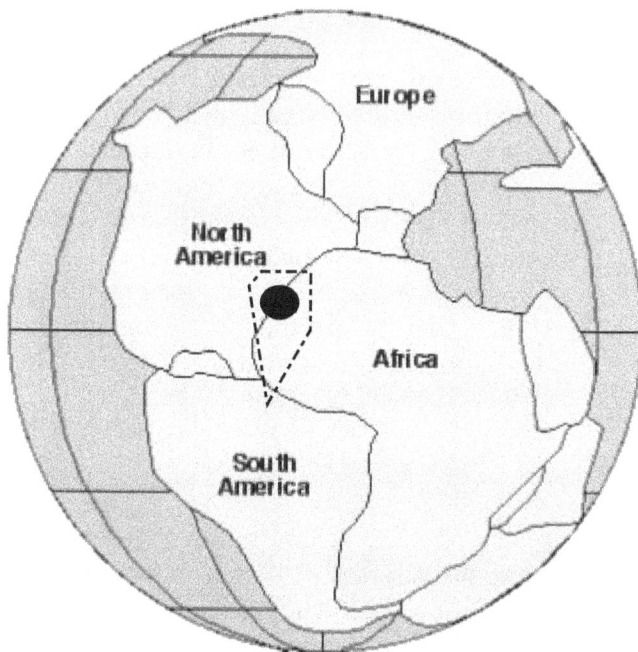

African tribal use of the fungus fairly matched that of their North American counterparts, though the Africans used it much more extensively. Besides being utilized for shamanic spirit journeys, it was used more practically as a remedy for gangrene and to heal cuts and wounds. It was also used nefariously as a poison at times, since the tiny seeds were easily mixed into food or drink and consumption usually went unnoticed by the victim.

35

The most common use of Devil's Snuff was as an ingredient in Conjure Bags (also called Hoodoo bags or Mojo Hands). Mojo is a small sack of various ingredients mixed by the shaman in order to bring forth magical results. Devil's Snuff when used as a hex was usually mixed with other organic compounds and placed underneath the victim's front steps, or buried in the hexee's back yard. Some cultures thought it prevented the victim from leaving his home, while others thought that it attracted evil spirits to the dwelling. Still others thought that when the victim crossed the threshold of the doorway, his mind would be confused and could be ultimately turned into a zombie slave belonging to whomever placed the hex.

This belief crossed over the Atlantic when African slaves were brought to the Southern states to work the plantations and farms. Slaves brought from West Africa and the West Indies were surprised to find the Devil's Snuffbox growing in the New World. Rootworkers (the hoodoo men and women who knew how to mix up conjure bags) put it to use much like they did in the old country, as a medicine and as a fetish. Small doses were mixed into cakes containing wheat, honey and a dove's heart for use as a love potion and given away to potential husbands or wives. Some wore their mojo bag around their necks as a ward against poisoning.

One story from Afro-American folklore makes great use of the Devil's Snuff. One of America's earliest "urban legends," the story of 'Chloe the house slave' was a cautionary tale designed to keep young slaves from aspiring to become a "house nigger" or to prevent them from trying to overly please the white man. The story has many variations (sometimes the slave's name is Cleo and the poison used is oleander or arsenic.) The tale is most commonly linked to Myrtle's Plantation in St. Francisville, Louisiana, but the repeated tellings of the same basic plot are so widespread that the legend may have originated in Africa, long before the slave trade even existed.

According to the legend, Chloe (or Cleo) was a house slave who fought off her Master's sexual advances. Other variations have Chloe listening in through the keyhole of a door and overhearing a secret, illegal business transaction between her Master and his accomplice. Either way, the result is the same: Chloe's ear is cut off and she is forced to wear a green turban to cover the wound.

Chloe then bakes a cake with the dove's heart, honey, wheat and Devil's Snuff mixture in order to regain the love of her Master and his family, who always treated her well prior to the ear-cutting incident. Other variations say that she planned to mildly poison the Master or his family, and then nurse them back to health, when they would once again show her compassion for saving their lives. (Other variants are even more straightforward: she baked the cake out of revenge and fully intended on poisoning her Master.)

Along the way, something goes wrong and only the Master's wife and children eat the cake, which kills them. Chloe is immediately suspected of the deed, and she runs off into the fields in hopes that her fellow slaves will hide her from certain death at the hands of her master. Instead, the other slaves lynch her, so that their Master will not punish them for Chloe's betrayal. (Other versions state that the hanging was done solely to gain favor from their Master, or to spare Chloe the torture that she would have likely endured before being executed.)

All versions of the tale end the same way: the ghost of a light-skinned black woman wearing a green turban and white dress can be seen haunting the grounds of the former plantation, mourning her accidental killing of the wife and two children, whom she loved dearly. Or, it's possible that she's still searching for her Master, in order to serve him a special cake...

**********

Sparse growth of the Devil's Snuffbox in the north didn't stop it from being used by African and Caribbean immigrants in New York and New Jersey. Among the burgeoning Jazz and Calypso music scene of the 1940's and '50's, many of the voodoo superstitions were taken just as seriously as they were in the old country. As the immigrants from Jamaica, Haiti, Trinidad and the Caribbean

# Observations
## on the Practice of Conjuring in Georgia

"I was conjured last May, 1898. I felt the first pain, hoeing in the field. It struck me in the right foot, and rested in my head. I went home, and knew I was conjured.

I looked for the conjure, found a little bag under my front doorstep, containing graveyard dirt, some night-shade roots, and some devil's snuff. I took the bag and dug a hole in the middle of the public road, where people walked, and I buried the bag, and sprinkled red pepper and sulphur in my house.

I have used fresh urine, pepper, and salt to rub with; am going to get fresh pokeberry root on the next new moon, make a tea, and rub with it. My feets feels hot, the conjure done put a fire in them."

— Interview with Negro farmhand, South Georgia.

Excerpted from the article OBSERVATIONS ON THE PRACTICE OF CONJURING IN GEORGIA by Roland Steiner. From the **Journal of American Folklore** magazine, Volume 14, 1900.

# SNUFFING WITH THE DEVIL

## BY JIM WALTER

As a writer, I was taught to know my subject well before I wrote about it. When Rob and I collaborated on this article, he wondered if it was possible to purchase Devil's Snuff anywhere.

A quick call to a number of African "medicine shops" in his town revealed that almost all of them stocked Devil's Snuff; the *real* Devil's Snuff, not the puffy mushroom crap that hippies eat.

A week later, I opened a package containing what looked like black pepper. I wanted to try it, but I didn't know how much of a dose to take. I did a little bit of research on the internet and found that approximately six seeds was enough to produce psychoactive results, and double that amount was potentially fatal.

I played it safe and carefully extracted five grains. (This required the use of a high-powered magnifying glass and some Revlon-brand tweezers). I called a friend over to make sure that if I started to die, he would be there to notify the authorities.

I snuffed the five grains directly off of the white piece of paper I had placed them on. Nothing happened. I sat back for about twenty minutes and felt a nice warming sensation at the base of my spine.

I went back and extracted three more grains and snuffed those, and this time I felt as though I was losing control of my body functions. My speech became slurred, and my vision blurry. My friend's hand was moving around, and it left faint "ghost" trails in the air for a few seconds before disappearing altogether. I sat down and attempted to watch television, but I couldn't focus. I turned on my laptop and attempted to write down what I was feeling, but I didn't have the energy.

After about twenty five minutes, I had returned to normal. No traces of the drug seemed to remain in my body.

It should go without saying that you should not attempt to recreate my experience, as it's very likely that you could die as a result. But I felt that it was a necessary thing to do in order to understand the mythology behind this famous fungal goofer dust. I'm still alive, and I'm not a zombie. Yet...

Islands poured in to Ellis Island, they brought with them their magical folk remedies and superstitions.

Hailing from Trinidad, Lord Invader quite clearly believed that jealous performers were not above trying to vex him with gris-gris and hexes. He once defiantly cried from the stage that "God made me impervious to Necromancy! Woe unto those that attempt to molest the me!"

Regardless, Lord Invader passed from this realm a short two years later. Was it really a simple heart attack, as the paperwork indicates, or was he the victim of a jealous necromancer? We'll probably never know for sure.

Had Lord Invader lived just a few years longer, who would have witnessed the Calypso music craze that was spearheaded by the likes of Harry Belafonte, who often used some of Lord Invader's music and lyrics in his own work (without bothering to give credit.) Maybe he could have even been a star, who knows?

One thing is certain though. Over fifty years after his death, people are still listening to his music, and idiots like Jim Walter are still using the Devil's Snuff. ᴴᵀᴱ

### FURTHER READING

- *Etnolologiska Studier* - S. Henry Wassen, 1965
- *Conjure in African American Society* - Jeffrey E. Anderson, 2007
- *Dictionary of English Plant Names* - William Miller, 1884
- *Calypso Calaloo* - Donald R. Hill, 1993

# STRANGE... BUT TRUE !

## TOBACCO-RELATED ODDITIES AND ANECDOTES

### COMPILED BY DAVID THIGPEN

## Butts For Fags

During the second World War, Great Britain was on financial life support. Their reserves were drained fighting the Nazis for what seemed an eternity. Munitions were getting hard to come by, let alone creature comforts like coffee, tobacco and shaving equipment.

At first, England turned to the US (who had still not entered the war yet) and France, who were happy to send supplies to the front line. Lucky Strike cigarettes, as described by a British soldier, were like "Manna from heaven."

But as Allied countries began to get lean on resources, the tobacco donations began to dwindle until the British had nothing to smoke. Whereas their previous rations were doled out in different increments (2 cartons of cigarettes per week, 32 ounces of pipe tobacco, or 16 ounces of snuff per week), the new tobacco rations rule cut those amounts in half. To add insult to injury, most squadrons didn't receive any of their rations due to shortages.

One thing that British soldiers did begin to receive in their packs were bakelite cigarette holders. Soldiers were confused as to why they had cigarette holders but no cigarettes, until Great Britain unveiled their new plan: stub cut cigarettes.

Stub cuts were packs of cigarettes that were cut in half on an assembly line with a repeating guillotine blade. The cigarettes were so small that they were nearly impossible to smoke without a holder.

Pretty soon, even the "halvsies" were gone. England's new strategy was to sweep up and collect spent cigarette butts from PX movie theatres. They were blended together into what was essentially a giant blender and re-manufactured into new cigarettes. These "floor sweepings" were tied together ten to a bundle with a thin silk string. These bundles of white sticks were called "faggots," then later just "fags." (*Faggot* at that time meaning a bundle of kindling wood tied together with a rope, and not a slur against homosexuals.)

On the homefront, the British Government began an unsuccessful campaign dubbed (don't laugh) "Butts for Fags", which urged citizens to save their discarded cigarette butts so that they could be recycled into new cigarettes. The resulting product was so wretched that soldiers refused to smoke them. Some of them ground the cigarettes into snuff to make it a bit more palatable.

Soon enough, the war would be over and the British troops were able to come home and get the Players and Craven A cigarettes they so gallantly deserved.

STE

# THE UNITED STATES GOVERNMENT

Well, it's been a busy month for political scandals here in the USA. We're only going to talk about two of them though, the two that directly effect this magazine, and by extension, our readers.

The illegal tapping by our friends at the Justice Department was the first "Huh?" incident that hit our desks this week. It seems that members of the Associated Press were targeted by the Justice Department, the legislative arm of the Executive Branch (ie, Obama's "public" Secret Service.)

The exact reason for the email traces, monitored surveillance, and wiretapped phonelines is still unclear. Vague whispers of the Benghazi scandal and "terrorist intel" have been put forth, but no concrete reason has been offered as of yet.

As three of our staff writers belong to the Associated Press, we feel that we have the right to know who, when, and where these taps occurred. We'd also like to know what information, if any, may have been compromised. After all, we've written about the Middle East before. Hell, we even had a picture of Bin Laden in one issue.

While I seriously doubt that we (the STE) were being secretly tracked, we'd love to know for sure, in writing, exactly how far this illegal overreach of governmental excess went. Is Jim Walter being followed by G-Men because of his "Nobama" bumper sticker? Will I have my phone tapped because I've stated several times that the US Government should be overthrown by the people in a bloody Revolution our forefathers implored us to start if things ever went the way they've ended up? We don't know. Every email we've sent to the JD with these questions has been answered with a form letter. Apparently a lot of other folks are worried they're on Obama's shit list as well.

CONT.

Clockwise from top: **Steve Miller**, former head of the Internal Revenue Service and author of such songs as "Fly Like an Eagle," "Rock'n Me" and "The Joker." As acting director of the IRS, he was aware that possibly conservative groups were being illegally mishandled by the IRS. Forced to resign, he has been caught in **over three dozen lies** before and after testifying before congress.

**Sarah Hall Ingram.** The bitch that once oversaw the IRS "hot seat," who actively encouraged IRS workers to harass and plague "conservatively themed" and "pro-Israel" tax exempt group status applications while working for the IRS during 2009-2012, was neither fired, nor forced to resign from her post. Too late, she's the overseeing director of **Obama's Affordable Care Act!** (That's Obamacare, for you college kids out there.) If she isn't in prison by the end of the year then the most unfathomable degree of federal corruption since Watergate (which this scandal easily surpasses in terms of Federal subterfuge) has taken place and a call to arms should be issued to the public by anyone who cares about all that is good and holy.

CLOCKWISE FROM TOP:

STEVE MILLER,

SARAH HALL INGRAM,

JOE "BIG DADDY" BIDEN,

A ZOMBIE,

LOIS LERNER,

ERIC HOLDER,

THE ANTICHRIST

On to the other scandal. In case you haven't heard, the Internal Revenue Service (the supposedly politically neutral collector of taxes for the Federal Government) has been caught targeting conservative and libertarian groups with illegal and unwarranted scare tactics.

Here's a true story: once upon a time (in 2010) a young man applied for 501c (3) tax exempt status for two non-partisan tobacco-rights groups: ASTRO (American Smokeless Tobacco Rights Organization) and AESTRO, (American/European Smokeless Tobacco Rights Organization).

The man was shocked when the paperwork arrived in a four inch thick Priority Mail envelope that was literally busting at the seams. "Gee," he thought to himself, "Mrs. Gardiner across the street had a ten-page application to fill out to start her gardening committee."

When the young man read through all 112 pages of legalese, he began filling out all of the pertinent information that the government asked of him. Some of the questions were kind of odd, but he answered them anyway with "NOYGDB," which he politely explained on the attached coversheet as being an acronym for "None Of Your God Damned Business." It looked a bit like this:

- How tall are you?  **6'1"**

- Who did you vote for in the last election, if you voted?  **NOYGDB**

- Would you consider yourself a republican, a democrat, or an independent? **NOYGDB**

- Who do you plan on voting for in the next election? **NOYGDB**

- Has anyone in your family ever served in the military? **YES**

- What was his/her branch of service and final rank obtained? **Army, General**

- Name of military family member? **E. Lee, Robert**

- Your hair color? **Grey, if I have to keep answering these questions. Currently dark brown.**

**Joe Biden,** the man who knows nothing yet can't keep his damned mouth shut.

**Hillary Clinton,** who as Secretary of State was aware of all of these scandals. Right now she's too busy covering her ass in Benghazi to be trifled with little things like illegal wiretapping and Felonious Federal F-ups.

**Lois Lerner**, who stepped into Sarah Ingram's post as director of Tax-Exempt applications at the IRS. After confessing to ABC News's Tom Costello that she coerced her subordinates into targeting potential conservative groups, he asked for a rough percentage of victims. After Costello named some numbers, Lerner asked "What is that, is that a quarter? **I'm not good with math.**" That's right. The top dog of the most abused department of the Internal Revenue Service is "not good with math." Even the normally reserved Costello was caught off guard. "But... you're with the IRS," he noted. She explained that she was a lawyer, not a mathematician. Then she apologized and figured this little snafu was all over with.

And so on went the questioning. The young man provided nearly 20 years worth of documents which meant that when he mailed back his applications, he had to do it via Media Mail in a large cardboard box. The contents had to have weighed at least 12 pounds!

After receiving a polite note stating that his applications had been accepted and were up for review, the young man would receive further notice by mail. Guess what?

## The young man was me, RW Hubbard, and I've been waiting three and a half years for my applications to be "processed."

That's right. I did this when I was a naive 27 year old that realized that even though the government was crooked, at least I could count on the IRS to play fair while they were stealing my money every year. Now I'm a bitter 31 year old man who has been audited three times since I applied for Tax Exempt status. (Last year, it was determined that I owed 7.00 in back taxes. Maybe they're hoping that one day I'll owe an entire ten dollar bill. )

So when the IRS scandal broke, I understand now why I never heard anything back. All 400 pages of crap that they required probably went into the shredder as soon as they read my cover letter.

For those of you who don't believe me, I was bitching about this on Snuscentral back in '09. Apparently my non-partisan tobacco collective was just too "tea party" for the IRS and so POOF! It disappeared. Numerous follow up emails and phone calls achieved nothing.

Everything that you've been hearing has been true. Yes, the applications were 100-200 pages long. Yes, they asked stupid questions like "what is the combined weight of you and your spouse?" or "How many miles per gallon do you think that your car gets on the highway? In the city?"

But you know what? I'm glad for it. If it wasn't for the IRS being a bunch of leftist whackjobs, there may not have ever been a Snuff Taker's Ephemeris. While ASTRO/AESTRO was in the planning stages, the STE was to be nothing but a mere newsletter. Now, thanks to you, it's the best tobacco magazine on the stands. STE

**Attorney General Eric Holder**, head of the Justice Department. This is the man that knows what your family had for dinner last night and which naked cam girl you clicked on back in 2002. He doesn't even have the balls to address the issue of the Justice Department's illegal AP drill, and there's no mention of it on the Justice Department's website whatsoever, even though thousands of Americans are calling for his resignation, if not a jail sentence.

Finally, we have the Prince of Lies himself. There's not much need to explain **Obama's** role in all of this except to say:
- Yes, he knew about it all.
- Yes, he was in a position to stop it.
- No, he has not done anything to the officials involved in these felonious activities, and likely never will. Politics make strange, crooked, worthless, evil bedfellows. STE

# Creepy Snuff Paraphenalia of the Month Award

## JACK THE RIPPER BRAND TOBACCO

Aaah, the good old days. Back when serial killers had their own tobacco named after them.

Jack the Ripper was an American brand of pouch tobacco, which meant it could be smoked when dried, or chewed right out of the bag, or ground up into snuff. We have no idea what company put this brand out, but it appeared on the market while the Ripper killings were still occurring in England.

According to the tag art, Jack the Ripper was some type of Neanderthal, which would explain his murderous tendencies. We're just trying to understand how a Neanderthal survived alongside humankind during the entire 5,000 years we've been on this earth?

STE

## "Priseur"

### A MALE SNUFF TAKER

(FRENCH, LATIN, SPANISH, SWEDISH, DANISH, DUTCH)

## "Priseuse"

### A FEMALE SNUFF TAKER

(FRENCH, LATIN, SPANISH, SWEDISH, DANISH, DUTCH)

# William Zantzinger

## "The Most Hated Tobacco Baron Since Buck Duke"

### A Look Back at The Life of a Man by RW Hubbard

*"William Zanzinger killed poor Hattie Carroll / With a cane that he twirled 'neath his diamond ring finger..."*

So begins "The Lonesome Death of Hattie Carroll," a song penned by Bob Dylan that appeared on his 1964 album *The Times They Are A-Changing*. If not for his topical ballad, the world today may not know the details of the William Zantzinger murder case that still sends ripples of rage throughout the collective spines of critics of the American Justice system.

Dylan wrote the song while returning from Martin Luther King's August 28th, 1963 "I Have A Dream" speech in Washington, DC. While leafing through the New York Times, Dylan came across an article about Zantzinger, who had been acquitted of First Degree Murder charges, coincidentally enough that same day. According to legend, Dylan sat up all night at a New York coffee shop and wrote the lyrics to the song, which described in deep, poetic detail the events that occurred in a "Baltimore Hotel society gathering" on February the 8th, 1963.

Above Right: *William Zantzinger being led to his trial for the murder of Hattie Carroll (next page).*

*Right:* Baltimore Afro-American, *Feb. 10 1963*

### Baltimore Afro-American

## MATRON FELLED BY CANE IN 'OLD PLANTATION' SETTING

Target's Weaver, not Adam Powell

*Freed On Bail*

*Rites Are Set*

Socialite charged, then state allows him $25,000 bail

Wilma still won't talk

'Something wrong with our city...'

Miss. is called

At the Spinster's Ball, wealthy tobacco farmer and well-known Baltimore socialite William "Billy" Zantzinger arrived drunk at about 9:00 PM with his wife Jane helping to prop him up. The 24 year old aristocrat of German descent was dressed mockingly in a giant top hat and was carrying a 25 cent wooden cane that he had won earlier that night in a carnival game.

Upon entering the Emerson hotel, the 6'2", 170 pound Zantzinger attacked the black bellhop that held the door open for him, for reasons that were never made clear. A friend of Zantzinger saw the scuffle and quickly escorted the drunk young man away from the fracas.

As the evening went on, Zantzinger's mood began to change from angry to happy. But a slow-moving black waitress soon drew his ire when she failed to serve him a drink as quickly as he thought she should have. Witnesses recall hearing Zantzinger shouting "you black bitch" or "you nigger" before jumping up and striking her with his fist (or with his cane; reports differ.)

By midnight he was thoroughly stewed, and he then turned his attention to the 51 year old barmaid that was busy serving the after-hours drinks. Zantzinger was heard calling her various derogatory names for the next hour and a half, in addition to throwing empty glasses at her for "not moving fast enough."

At about 1:30 AM, with most of the attendees having gone home for the night, Zantzinger leaned against the bar and called for a bourbon. "Hey black bitch," he called Hattie Carroll, the aforementioned barmaid, "hey you black son of a bitch." Mrs. Carroll tried to mix the drink as quickly as possible to avoid having the man yell at her even more. But apparently it wasn't fast enough for Mr. Zantzinger, who climbed across the bar shouting "nigger" and striking Hattie Carroll with his cane in her head and on her shoulders.

His wife pulled him from off of the bar and tried to calm him down, but Zantzinger slapped her so hard that she fell to the ground. His wife nearly unconscious, he then took off his shoe and started hitting her in the face with it until some of the guests were able to pull him off of her.

Hattie Carroll reeled back from the assault and into the arms of a fellow barmaid. She was dizzy and out of breath. "I feel deathly ill," Hattie said. "That man... has upset me so."

The barmaid helped her into the kitchen, where she complained about her arm being numb. Her speech then dissolved into a nonsensical babble and Hattie lapsed into a state of unconsciousness. An ambulance was called and Hattie was rushed to the hospital. The mother of 11 died about eight hours later, from what the autopsy report showed was a brain hemorrhage.

William Zantzinger was arrested for first degree murder the following day and taken in to custody. He made the $600 bail easily enough and returned to his Charles County farm until trial. With the "most expensive lawyers that his father could buy," Zantzinger's defense pleaded that Billy was just a simple farm boy, not used to the ways of the big city. He drank too much (poor boy) and unfortunately took it out on Mrs. Carroll, who was serving drinks after hours anyway and had high blood pressure and hard-

ened arteries.

*Maybe* if Mrs. Carroll had taken better care of herself, and *maybe* if Mrs. Carroll hadn't been in criminal neglect by illegally serving alcohol after midnight to this poor, naive country boy, and *maybe* if she would have not intentionally angered the poor boy by deliberately "moving too slow" after being called a "nigger" and a "bitch" (Mrs. Carroll was the president of a negro social club, so she probably harbored racial predjudice against the farm boy) repeatedly, *maybe* William Zantzinger wouldn't have been provoked into striking her with his little toy cane and *maybe* Mrs. Hattie Carroll wouldn't have coincidentally suffered a brain hemorrhage just moments later, brought on by her poor health habits.

*Maybe*, the lawyers contended, this whole sorry affair could have been avoided. As it stood, their client was just as much a victim of circumstance as the unfortunate Hattie Carroll, who was at least partially responsible for her own demise, and Billy should be given an apology from the people of Baltimore for the smearing of the good name of the Zantzinger family.

The judge was sympathetic, and reduced the charge of Murder in the First Degree to that of Manslaughter. In what can only be described as a sheer middle finger in the face of the American judicial process, Zanzinger didn't even face a sentencing jury to determine his punishment. Instead, he stood before three district court judges that sternly sentenced the murderer to six months in jail and a $500 fine. (He was also fined $125, separately, for the assault on the bellhop.)

Zantzinger was to serve his time in the Washington County Jail, as opposed to the State Prison, where it was feared that retaliation from black inmates would jeopardize Zantzinger's safety. Seeing that Zantzinger was such a good lad, the judges even deferred his sentence for six months so that he could tend to that year's tobacco harvest.

While leaving his home to begin his stay in the county jail, a remorseful Zantzinger told the press that the only thing he was going to miss while he was away from his farm was "just a bunch of snow."

"It's a shame," his wife said. "Nobody treats his negroes as well as Billy does around here." Zantzinger served five of the six months in jail; he was released early for good behavior.

While the case didn't reach the same level of publicity that similar white on black murders like the Emmet Till and Medgar Evers cases did, the public that *was* aware of it reeled from the impact of this blatant miscarriage of justice. Calls for a retrial fell mostly on deaf ears.

Zantzinger returned to his family farm and resumed tobacco production. Eventually, the notoriety of the case caused him to seek life in the big city, where he could hide himself from the prying eyes of the press and the media. He moved to Waldorf, Maryland and began selling real estate.

All through his life, Zantzinger was plagued by the repeated intrusions on his privacy from curious writers and filmmakers that sought his side of the story after being made aware of the case from Dylan's song. He scoffed at the notion that his family connections and wealth kept him out of jail. "My daddy only served one damned term in the state legislator. That bastard [Bob Dylan] is a damned liar and I should have sued his sorry tail and put him in jail," he said in a 1991 interview. Conversely, he said ten years later that the song "actually had no effect on my life," though he still harbored an unbridled grudge for Bob Dylan. "He's a no-account son of a bitch, he's just like a scum of a... scum bag of the earth, I should have sued him and put him in jail."

He would go on to divorce his first wife and marry again, to a woman named Suzanne Howard. He was known to his friends as a charitable and decent man, giving money to churches and schools (the same schools that just a few years earlier he denounced by saying "Hell, you wouldn't want to go to school with Negroes any more than you would with French people.")

But trouble seemed to follow Billy throughout the rest of his life, no matter how hard he tried to give back to his fellow man. In 1990, he was convicted of being a slum lord and for illegally renting out properties that weren't up to living standards. He paid a $5,000 fine and apologized to the court.

The very next year he was arrested for illegal collection of rent on properties he no longer possessed. Zantzinger once owned a string of tenant shacks that were condemned five years earlier for not meeting living standards. Ever the humanitarian, Zantzinger installed running water and electricity to the 25 poverty shacks (all occupied by black families) but failed to pay the $65,000 in fines and back taxes he owed the state county. The state seized his homes and ordered the occupants to move out. Zantzinger told his renters that it was all a mix-up in paperwork and allowed them to continue living there, collecting rent on the properties that he no longer owed.

This went on for about five years before his scheme was discovered, and he was again arrested and ordered to serve 18 months in the county jail. He was also made to serve 2400 hours of community service and to take part in community programs that were intended to help poor blacks find a way out of slum life.

Almost thirty years after his first jail sentence, Zantzinger finally publicly apologized for one of his transgressions. "I never intended to hurt anyone, ever, ever. It's not my nature, I got into this hole, dug it. It was my mistake. It got deeper and deeper. I've learned my lesson, believe me."

During the 90's, Zantzinger turned into a foreclosure auctioneer. Instead of collecting rent on condemned shacks, Zantzinger would go around the state scoping out dilapidated properties, researching the owners, and "flipping" the property over to other investors.

Sometimes these houses were made barely livable and rented out to poor minorities. Others were (thankfully) torn down and existing land re-appropriated for other purposes.

"I learned my lesson, believe me." Zantzinger in 1991.

Zantzinger passed away on January 10th, 2009, aged 69, of natural causes. We at *The Ephemeris* have attempted to reach out to his family for the last two years for their take on the life of their patriarch. We finally received a response from a representative of the family who said that "we have no use for the way the media has twisted the facts for years now and we have nothing else to say."

As for Hattie Carroll's family, her great-granddaughter Talya stated that the murder tore her family apart. Several of Hattie's children became involved in the civil rights movement, some joining the Black Panther party and some becoming devout followers of the Nation of Islam. This seemed to cause a rift with the older conservative Baptists in the Carroll family. The family split into different factions and the division between brothers, cousins, aunts and uncles has never healed.

When we spoke with Ms. Carroll, she was unaware that Zantzinger had passed away. "I would have liked to have been at his funeral. I would have loved to have been there to spit on his grave."

STE

# Swedish Match Svenskt Snus Store and Lounge: Counting Down...

*All of a sudden, the concept of "Ye Olde Corner Pub" just got a hell of a lot more exciting.*

# By Larry Waters

Saturday, 01 December 2012

*Name your poison: fresh fruit, baked pies, artisan lemonade, or a big bowl of Grov.*

*Interactive General Snus Exhibit.*

**Stockholm** - At 11:00 AM (GMT+1), less than an hour and a half from now as I begin writing, Swedish Match AB will officially open their Snus Store/Snus Experience/Snus Museum/Cappuccino Bar etc. at Kungsgatan 3 in Stockholm. Lars Dahlgren, CEO of SMAB will be on hand to welcome guests and answer questions. If you are an American visiting Stockholm today, you may want to drop by, have your picture taken with Lars, and ask him why General Onyx and Grovsnus Svart, both black portion snus brands sold in the US for years, have been absent most of 2012 for what I'm told is a black dye issue with FDA.

If that is in fact the issue, perhaps he could "encourage" the SM R&D Team in Gothenburg to prioritize a solution.

If it is a regulatory issue, perhaps someone in Legal could explain (so even I can understand) why two snuses which were grandfathered in as pre-PACT Act/pre-Tobacco Control Act brands suddenly are considered new products to FDA.

I would ask him nicely though, since both General Onyx and Grovsnus Black will be available in the Stockholm store and you could stock up while visiting. The last thing you would want is to be banned from the store for acting like a soccer hooligan.

For Americans who have only recently discovered the wonder which is REAL Swedish snus, General Onyx Black Portion Snus is the very top of the line product in the General Snus brands. If General White Portion is a Chevrolet, Onyx is a Cadillac. It is a real treat for General Snus fans... Except that you can't order it from the US anymore.

One thing Mr. Dahlgren *will* be able to

offer you is fresh Swedish Match snus of all kinds; not just today but every day. The Swedish Match Snus Store will receive a brand new fresh inventory of snus every morning prior to the store opening. Any snus remaining from the day before will be removed from the store and returned to the factory.

If you see any Kardus Cincho 2012 on the shelves, grab it quickly. The SnusCentral Snus Shop ran out yesterday and there is no more is available. Only 600 boxes were produced as is the tradition with Kardus. This year's Kardus is not only very tasty, but rather high in nicotine. It's after 3 AM in my time zone and if I didn't have a large prilla of Kardus Cincho under my lip, I would have fallen asleep by now.

Marcus Carlsson, a very important person at Swedish Match, has been working feverishly with his team to prepare the snus store for the Grand Opening.... in about 45 minutes from now. I'm sure the Sunday Swedish newspapers will be full of details concerning the store I can't even begin to imagine. I look forward to reading all about today and getting a first hand narrative from

Marcus who will hopefully be relaxing on a beach somewhere by Monday.

Thanks to Marcus and the SnusCIA, you the reader will beat the public in seeing the interior of the Swedish Match Snus Store in Stockholm. These three interior photos of the store were taken about 14 hours ago and have not been released before now.

Congratulations to everyone at Swedish Match on this exciting Grand Opening. A visit is first on my list the next time I'm in Stockholm... if Lars hasn't permanently barred me because of the General Onyx incident.

Sorry. I'm working on an article about General Onyx so those questions were on the top of my mind. I'm also drinking heavily as I write this; a SnusCentral tradition both here in the Texas SnusCentral.org Bunker and in Lidköping at the SnusCentral.com Snus Store.

Time for a fresh prilla of Kardus Cincho and to get this article published before 11:00 AM in Stockholm.....2 minutes from now! STE

# We Want The Airwaves:
# The Ephemeris Attacks A Local Radio Station

### A conversation featuring RW Hubbard

*It's 4:13 am and I get a call from Bill Johnson. "Turn it on station W\*\*\*."*

*"What station is that?" I ask, since I'm not 83 and I don't listen to morning AM talk radio.*

*After finding the right station and taping my AM loop to the wall for reception, I'm listening to the largest pack of lies I've ever heard over the air concerning smokeless tobacco. It's some Air Force General bantering with a local DJ about how the armed forces need to completely ban smokeless tobacco from their bases. In fact, he states that by 2015 he would like to see all soldiers, marines, seamen, airmen and guardsmen completely nicotine free.*

*The discussion cuts to the commercial break and the DJ asks for anyone with an opinion to call in. I jot down the number and call the station immediately. A man with a lisp asks me who I am and what I want to talk about. "My name's Rob Hubbard and I publish* The Snuff Taker's Ephemeris, *the journal of smokeless tobacco, right here in Fayetteville."*

*"Oh gosh! This should be good. Keep it clean and wait for [the DJ] to introduce you. Make sure your radio is off and thank you for calling. Please stay on the line while I transfer you."*

*After about a minute, I hear noise on the other end of the line and hit "record" on my answering machine. "...publisher of the Snuff Taker's Ephe... Ephemeris? I don't know. Sounds fancy. But he's here to set the record straight on some of these things [Air Force Guy] has been saying, so says he. Thank you for calling Mr. Hubbard..."*

Me: Thank you for having me, or letting me call in or whatever. Call me Rob, please.

**DJ: It says here that you publish the only magazine... or periodical... devoted entirely to smokeless tobacco?**

Me: That's correct.

**DJ: So I imagine that you know your subject fairly well. It's not like there's a lot of guys that have PHD's in snuff or chewing tobacco.**

Me: [slight laugh] No, I suppose not. Just to get the name out, the magazine is entitled *the Snuff Taker's Ephemeris* and it's published here in Fayetteville, so I'm a local boy...

**DJ: And it's entirely about snuff? I'm looking at your website now and it's pretty... It's pretty classy looking.**

Me: Wait till you read a copy! It's a sleaze rag. [Laughs from all three of us.]

**DJ: So, getting back to what I was talking about with [AG-Airforce Guy], you probably have a different opinion about smokeless tobacco than he does.**

Me: Well, I have to admit that I missed the first few minutes of the show but for the last ten minutes... No, I can't say I agree with [him] at all. He's describing two, three, even ten and twenty year old studies that have been discredited...

**DJ: Discredited by who?**

Me: Well, besides myself and my writers, by "junk science" media watchdogs like Mike Siegel and Bill Godshall. Then on the actual science end you have people like Dr. Lars-Erik Rutqvist and Dr. Brad Rodu who have basically wiped their butts with these reports since day one. Nobody takes them seriously except the anti-tobacco extremists that wish to rid our military of tobacco use across the board.

AG: *Can I say something here?*

**DJ: Sure.**

AG: *These reports have been backed up by the American Cancer Society and the American Lung Association and have proven to be accurate. If I'm not mistaken, don't the doctors that you've cited receive funding money from big tobacco organizations?*

Me: Sure. And if I'm not mistaken, doesn't the ACS and the ALA receive funding from the big pharmaceutical companies like Pfizer?

AG: *I'm not aware, but it is possible, yes.*

**DJ: So basically what I'm hearing is that groups connected with tobacco companies have condemned the studies, while groups associated with the pharmaceutical companies have praised the reports? Is that what you're saying?**

Me: No, not at all. I cited two examples of scientists who receive funding from tobacco companies. These studies are routinely torn apart by people like me who have nothing to do with tobacco companies. I don't receive a stipend from the RJR or the PMI. Can [Air Force Guy] say the same about the American Cancer Society, the ALA, or any other anti-tobacco entity in operation?

**DJ: Does he receive backing from the anti-tobacco groups? Do you, AG?**

AG: *Some of the work we've built on has been in part, financed by special interest groups.*

Me: And? What are their names?

AG: *I don't have a complete list, but I do believe the ALA and ACS are in there.*

Me: So, what I'm gathering is that you're trying to discredit Drs. Rutqvist and Rodu because they receive funding from tobacco advocates, therefore making their work biased, while your researchers who are funded by anti-tobacco groups are squeaky clean. It doesn't go both ways. If you're going to discredit a source based on funding, then you have to take yourself and your studies off the table first.

**DJ: Sounds fair. But at the same time, I mean, the money has to come from somewhere...**

Me: Did you know that the doctors I just cited started out as researchers for anti-tobacco groups? When the American Cancer Study determined that their findings didn't match their agenda, that smokeless tobacco is not some horrible, dangerous killer, they cut their funding. So being intrigued by their findings, the tobacco companies stepped in and allowed them to continue their research by continuing their funding. So it's not like Big Tobacco knocked on their doors one day and said "we need you to make up some studies that skew the truth." In fact, these guys were essentially fired from Big Anti-Tobacco foundations because they didn't like the truth that was coming out of the research.

**DJ (to AG): What have you got to say for that?**

AG: *As far as those incidents, and I am aware of that particular situation, these studies have nothing to do with those.*

Me: Why not? They were written by the same discredited authors and funded by the same organizations that attempted to "buy" cooked studies that show non-harmful tobacco products to be more dangerous than they really were. Am I right?

AG: *I really don't know, because you can't name any of these organizations that have backed the study.*

Me: I'm online now, hold on. Yep, funded in part by The ACS, The ALA and.. oh my god... the Legacy Campaign?

**DJ: What is the Legacy plan?**

Me: They're those stupid "Truth" commercials you've seen on television where teenagers pile up body bags of dead smokers in front of "big tobacco headquarters."

**DJ: Ah. What's wrong with them?**

Me: Everything. [Laughs.] They were created as part of the Master Settlement so they're basically funded by tobacco money reaped by the federal government. Once smoking rates went down they turned their sights on smokeless and run ad after crooked ad that says stuff like "smokeless tobacco is just as dangerous as smoking" and crap like that.

**DJ: Is it?**

Me: Is smokeless as dangerous as smoking? Heck no. It's an actually scientifically calculated probability that smokeless tobacco is 98% safer than smoking. Study after study after study that has come out of Europe over the last 30 years paints the same picture: if you can't stop smoking, switch to smokeless tobacco. Preferably Swedish snus or nasal snuff, since these don't cause heart or lung problems and in the last 300 years have never been attributed to a single case of cancer.

**DJ: Are you serious? There's tobacco that doesn't effect the body negatively and the anti-tobacco groups want to ban it? Why?**

Me: That's a great question! I'd like [Air Force Guy] to answer that one.

AG: *Well, we're under the opinion-*

Me: Not your opinion, the facts. [Jack Webb voice]. Just the facts, sir. [Nervous laughter from DJ].

AG: *...based on our research, there is no such thing as healthy tobacco use. Snuff causes oral cancer, and there's no denying that. These other forms of tobacco you mention? Yes, I've heard that they're possibly safer but I haven't seen a convincing study to prove so yet.*

**DJ: Do you agree with that, Rob? That dip or chewing tobacco, the American kind anyways, can cause cancer?**

Me: Dip? Sometimes. Chewing tobacco? No. And here's why. For many years, American oral snuff was very high in TSNAs, which are the carcinogens most likely to cause mouth cancer. There have been people in the past who have succumbed to oral cancer from the use of such antiquated snuff. Chewing tobacco will rot your teeth due to all of the sugar, but it's so low in TSNAs that there's never been a link between it and oral cancer. So to answer your question, yes, I believe American smokeless products have caused cancer in the past. But now that they're basically manufactured like European smokeless tobacco products, the TSNAs are low and the cancer rate for American dippers is not statistically higher than it is for non-dippers, and it's been that way for at least ten years.

**DJ: What say you to that, General?**

AG: *I agree that oral cancer is not as prevalent as lung cancer, but it still effects a certain segment of the population.*

Me: Yeah, but that "certain segment" of the population that gets oral cancer... there's no difference between dippers and non-dippers. If you pick ten random oral cancer sufferers, five of them will be non-tobacco users and the other five will be dippers. There's no causal evidence to suggest that the five dippers got cancer from tobacco. You'll have to look at what all ten patients together have in common before you can start finding epidemiological behavior with the statistics to back up your theory.

**DJ: So, Rob, what you're saying is that every smoker in the world- right now- were to switch to smokeless, there would be no cancer?**

Me: No, there'd still be cancer. But smoking-related cancer would virtually disappear within the course of our children's lifetime.

**DJ: And this goal can't be achieved by nicotine drugs, like patches, and gum, or Chantix?**

Me: Not according to the evidence. Most people that try Nicotine Replacement Therapy like gum, patches and lozenges end up going back to smoking. 7 out of 10 smokers. Yet 7 out of 10 smokers that switch to smokeless tobacco stop smoking completely. And the risks are lower than NRT. You ever heard of anyone committing suicide while snuffing? It happens with Chantix. I was watching the news last night about the big lawsuit against Pfizer for putting Chantix on the market, knowing that it caused suicidal tendencies in some people. Now Pfizer is paying teens $800 to take part in studies where they're given Chantix to curb their smoking habit. They have to sign a waiver stating that Pfizer is not responsible for any misfortune, including suicide, that may be brought on in these clinical tests. Could you imagine RJ Reynolds getting away with that? 'Hey, underage smokers, try this snus and tell us if it helps you stop smoking Camels.' They'd be hung out to dry immediately, front page of every newspaper in the country. But the Pfizer study doesn't even rate fourth-page news.

**DJ: That's some scary stuff. [Airforce Guy], did you know about this?**

AG: *Not that particular study, no. But you have to understand that any time a drug goes on the market, it's still tested even if it has been in the market for a while. So that's what they're probably doing, is monitoring the behavior of patients on the medication.*

Me: Yet, the FDA is doing everything it can to block tobacco companies from marketing safe tobacco products as an alternative to smoking. Why is it so quick to demonize what science has proven to be safer and more effective than these pharmaceutical alternatives?

AG: *Well, you are under the impression that there are, firstly, "safe" tobacco products. There are no such things...*

DJ: **But according to what I'm reading right now online, and I'm sorry to interrupt your point [Airforce Guy], the Swedes have been studying snus, which I guess is their word for snuff, for decades and found that it doesn't cause cancer, doesn't cause heart disease, oral cancer, etc etc, so... I'm inclined to go with Mr. Hubbard here. How much safer do you want it? I'm looking at a page right now that says chewing gum is more dangerous than snus, and this was done at Harvard...**

AG: *Those studies are still not fully accepted by the medical community.*

Me: And the studies you cite are not accepted by anyone *outside* the medical community.

AG: *Well, we're working to change that...*

Me: How do you argue fact? How do you "change" facts? The only thing that points smokeless tobacco- and I'm talking modern products, even though snus has been around for 300 years- as being dangerous are studies that are easily ripped apart by any academian, yet the ones that show smokeless as being 98% safer than smoking are airtight. So the only alternative for people like you is to try and discredit the source, which you do whenever a study is funded by a tobacco company. Well, what about the studies that aren't founded, or I mean funded, by the tobacco companies? You choose to simply ignore them. It's hypocrisy.

DJ: **Fellas, this has turned out to be an interesting talk. What I'd like to do is to schedule the two of you for an on-air interview sometime so we can hash out more of these thoughts.**

Me: That would be excellent. [Airforce Guy agrees].

DJ: **I have to say, with all respect [Airforce Guy], that before you came on I was under the impression that if you chewed tobacco, then your mouth rotted off, no question. But just from what I've read in the last five minutes... And from what Mr. Hubbard has been saying... There's a whole other aspect to this that is not being publicized. I say this as a former smoker, one who smoked for thirty years, and tried to quit for the last twenty of those years [laughs]. And if I had known that there was an alternative like these snus dissolvables or whatever they are... It's possible I could have quit much sooner than I did. Just curious Robert, did you, or were you a smoker before you started using snus?**

Me: Absolutely. I smoked for 15 years, since I was 13. And I smoked non-filtered cigarettes, so if there was anyone that could be called "hooked to the gills" on smoking, it was me. And of course I tried the pharmaceutical alternatives, and like 75% of smokers who do, I simply went back to smoking. But when I discovered snus, that was when I quit. Cold turkey. Never looked back.

DJ: **That's just.. That's an incredible story. It's inspiring, you know, for people out there who think they might as well just keep smoking. What are.. what are your thoughts on.. people's experiences like that [Airforce Guy]?**

AG: *Well...*

DJ: **I mean, would you rather ban snus and he goes back to smoking and ends up with emphysema? What's your take on that?**

AG: *Firstly, I congratulate anyone who quit smoking. But I would love it if he was also tobacco-free to boot.*

Me: Because you don't like tobacco and you don't think anyone should use it.

AG: *Hold on...*

Me: That was once tried in this country with Prohibition. And it didn't work. This mentality of "I don't like it, so I want everyone to stop doing it altogether" is really the only thing holding the anti-tobacco activists crowd together.

DJ: **On that note, I'm going to have to say goodbye to our guests as we break for news and weather, but trust me, I'm sure we're going to hear more about this at another time.** [DJ goes on and thanks Airforce Guy and lists his credentials and thanks him for his service to our country.]

AG: *Thank you, [DJ].*

DJ: **And Robert Hubbard, publisher of The Snuff Taker's...**

Me: Ephemeris.

DJ: **Eph... Uh... Meeris. The Snuff Taker's Ephemeris. Jeez, couldn't you just call it the Snuff Taker's Magazine? [laughs]**

Me: [laughing] I could, but we'd sell more copies that way. We want to remain underground. Our website by the way is snuffmagazine.org. You can order from us or at Amazon.

DJ: **Can you buy this at your local bookstore?**

Me: Absolutely. If it's not in stock, they should be able to order it for you.

DJ: **Well thank you gentlemen. Well, it's quarter past... blah blah blah...**

*And that's basically where it ended. What's funny is that the guy with the lisp took down my information and told me that they would be in contact with me in the future to set up a panel discussion. This was in November 2012.*

*In February 2013, I contacted the radio station to check on the status of the follow-up interview, but was told that they hadn't scheduled anything. I also asked for permission to reprint the original chat in my magazine. I got a nice form email denying me permission to reproduce in whole or in part any transcript of "Billy Joe's Morning Cuppa Joe" and how they'll kill me if I infringe on their copyright, etc.*

*So I decided to print the transcript anyway, verbatim, just excluding the name of the station and the participants. So if nobody sees me in the next couple of weeks, it's because the copyright police snatched me up and took me to whatever concentration camps they put people who record Major League Baseball Games without express written permission of the MLB.*

STE

# AC vs DC

## The Shocking True Story of Two Snuffers And Their Battle for Electrical World Domination

Two men, one goal: modernizing the world through the invention of electricity. Over the years, myths, legends and misinformation have helped to mar the accomplishments of both of these innovators. In this article, we try to objectively define the contributions these men made to the world of science.

**Thomas Alva Edison**
Feb 11, 1847 - October 18, 1931

**Nikola Tesla**
July 10, 1856 - January 7, 1943

Thomas Alva Edison was born into a middle class family in Milan, Ohio. The family later moved to Port Huron, Michigan where Edison spent most of his early years. His father was a Canadian Reformer who fled to the US after his name was added to the list of "criminals" who took part in the Canadian Rebellions of 1838. (The revolutions were modeled after the American Revolution; intellectuals and working class Canadians were trying to replace the Monarchist government with a more Libertarian/ Republican democracy. Though the uprisings were both unsuccessful, they did eventually lead to the era of "responsible government," which like the age of American Constitutionalism, has largely been abandoned in favor of "progressive" Canadian idealism.)

Thomas Edison was a "fidgety" student, and left elementary school after only three months. He was home-schooled by his mother, mainly from the book *School of Natural Philosophy* by R.G. Parker. Heady reading for a third grader, indeed.

At the age of 14, he got his first job selling newspapers on the street corner. In what would be a foreshadowing of his entrepreneurial drive, Edison "hired" four other boys to sell the papers for him, with Edison keeping much of the profit. With this money he began producing his own newspaper, *The Grand Trunk Herald*, which he sold right alongside the other newspapers he hawked.

He then got a job working on a passenger train, selling his newspapers and other items like cigars and candy. This allowed him to purchase a chemistry set, which he would practice using during his long trips around the country. These experiments climaxed in an explosion inside an empty boxcar, and Edison was thrown off the train by the conductor, nearly a hundred miles from home. Edison hitchhiked the rest of the way back, rather than spend any money on a train ride. His spendthrift nature also prohibited him from visiting an ear doctor. His hearing was severely damaged during the explosion, and he gradually grew deafer the older he got. By the time he died, he was completely deaf.

At the age of 18, he had saved up enough money to open his own grocery stands throughout the city. The revenue was so good that he used the proceeds to open up a variety of companies, devoted to everything from medicine to physics and to electrical-mechanical enterprises. General Electric was the most successful of these businesses and is still one of the largest and most profitable companies in the world.

While still working for the railroad, Edison saved the life of three-year-old James Mackenzie, the son of a station agent. The boy had fallen onto the tracks, directly into the path of an oncoming train. Edison grabbed the boy and threw him to safety just as the train passed by. The boy's father was so thankful that he put Edison to work as a telegraph agent in Ontario, Canada.

His success in the field led to a full time job with Western Union in Louisville, Kentucky, working the Associated Press newswire. He chose the nightshift, which was usually slow-paced and allowed Edison to work on his inventions during the silent stretches. One night, while working on a new type of battery, he spilled some sulphuric acid on the floor, which ate through the wood floor and onto his boss's desk two stories below. Edison was fired the next morning.

Almost all of the profit that Edison incurred from his businesses were funneled back into more research. His concentration was mainly focused on telegraphy, and his first major invention was an improved stock ticker which would eventually make its predecessors obsolete.

Franklin Leonard Pope, a fellow inventor and telegraph enthusiast, took pity on the struggling young Edison and allowed him to live in the Pope family basement. This gave Edison the much-needed privacy and time to concentrate on more inventions. His first patent, for an electric voting booth, was granted on June 1st, 1869.

He would soon marry his first wife, 16 year old Mary Stillwell, who bore him three children. She died young, at age 29, from what was thought to be an undiagnosed brain tumor. Historians today believe that it was more likely from a morphine overdose. Records show that Mary Edison was prescribed a huge amount of the pain killer, even for that era, for menstrual cramps and migraine headaches. All of her symptoms prior to death are consistent with morphine poisoning.

Edison's first major invention was for the phonograph, the first device to play back recorded sounds. The phonograph recorded and played back sounds imprinted on a tinfoil cylinder. The invention shocked the public, who thought that sound recording was an impossibility. (The first recorded sound ever made was a 15 second track of Edison reciting the first verse of "Mary Had A Little Lamb," which still survives to this day.)

Edison took the profits from this invention (as well his sale of the rights to the quadruplex telegraph, which he sold to Western Union for $10,000) and used them to build the world's first industrial complex in Menlo Park, New Jersey. The pressed soon dubbed him "The Wizard of Menlo Park."

Throughout the rest of his career, Edison invented minor projects here and there that were completely original in design. But the bulk of Edison's 1,000-plus patents were for ideas (like the quadruplex telegraph) that he improved upon from earlier inventions. His next major patent was for the carbon microphone which was used in all telephones until the early 1980s. But the only thing "new" about the microphone was that it was made from carbon; its design was copied almost directly from Emil Berliner's earlier telephone transmitter microphone, a patent that was later dismissed as part of the decade-long "telephone wars" of the 1870's and 80's. A device created by an immigrant Jew that was declared "derivative" one year was touted as "highly original" when presented by The Wizard of Menlo Park a few years later.

Thus began Edison's long descent into plagiarism and back-stabbing. His employees would often develop new inventions which Edison would buy outright and patent himself, taking all due credit for its conception in the process. He once explained to Lewis Latimer, an inventor under his employ, that once a man sold his patent and kept the initial proceeds, it would take that inventor years of business acumen to keep profiting from the invention. He had to continually modify it to make it more efficient and avoid becoming obsolete.

Edison was almost doing a favor to these inventors by buying them out and allowing them to continue working for him (with a salary raise, to boot) rather then letting them end up penniless. Edison was being downright noble in his actions, according to his own philosophy. This was hard to explain to a man making ten dollars a week who just sold his invention to Edison for a couple of thousand dollars, while Edison raked in millions in turn.

Edison's next invention was the incandescent lightbulb. Though many lightbulbs existed prior to Edison's, Edison did the same trick he pulled with the carbon telephone microphone and replaced the metal filament with one made from carbon, which had a longer life and shone brighter than previous designs. There was only two problems; the work was "highly derivative" of earlier designs and less than a year earlier, a British patent was awarded to Joseph Swan for the same exact lightbulb. Edison was denied a patent in his own country and his bulb would not have been marketable in England due to Swan's own patent. He then partnered with Swan and formed the company "Edswan" which marketed the bulb in Europe. (Edison was eventually awarded the patent after six years of litigation by a judge with close relations to one of the financial backers of the Menlo Park Industrial Complex.)

Now that Edison could profit from his electrical lamp, he needed a way to profit from the *energy* that it took to light the bulbs. He began diverting his research team towards Direct Current generators, and by January 1882 had constructed the first steam-powered generator house in London. The gen-

*"What, this lightbulb? Yeah, I invented it. What do you mean "improved" upon? Let me show you this new "improved" quadruplex shotgun I've been working on. It has four barrels instead of two."*

erator provided several homes within a two block radius with electrical light and also powered the first electrical streetlights. People came from all over England to witness the spectacle of the "flameless candle."

Edison then founded the international Edison Illuminating Company, which had offices all over the US and Europe. With investor backing, Edison opened his Pearl Street station, which supplied power to 59 customers in lower Manhattan.

Electrical power was sure to be the wave of the future, and for the time being Edison held a monopoly on its use in England and the US. He charged a hefty fee for his customers; only the wealthiest were able to upgrade to Direct Current indoor illumination.

All of this work caught the ear of a Serbian inventor and electrical enthusiast who began a correspondence with Edison over theoretical design improvements which would greatly improve the efficiency of Edison's generators. Edison was impressed by the young man's enthusiastic ideas and offered him a job at the French branch of the Continental Edison Company. That man's name was Nikola Tesla.

If ever there was a genius to walk the face of the earth, it was Nikola Tesla. Tesla was a Serb, the son of a minister in the Serbian Orthodox Church. The area that he was born in was later incorporated into Croatia, causing many Croatians to claim that he was in fact a Croat and not a Serb. (It is an undisputable fact that Tesla was Serbian and not Croatian, but many Croats still insist on claiming him as "one of their own.")

He did quite well all throughout school and it is quite possible that he had a photographic memory. He was able to work out long, complicated calculus formulas in his head, making many of his teachers believe that he was somehow cheating at his schoolwork.

As a child, he had already started working on electrical contraptions. His first invention was a rotary engine that was powered by the friction caused by the movement of 16 junebugs. The experiment failed when his mildly retarded friend opened the motor and ate the junebugs.

After graduating high school and battling a nearly fatal bout of cholera, his father placed him in the Austrian Polytechnic in Graz, Austria, where he had earned a scholarship. He finished four years of work within a two-year period and was often asked to stand in as a substitute professor when needed.

It is quite clear now that Tesla suffered from OCD, and was known to work 60 hours a week without sleep until he could solve whatever problems were vexing him. He soon became a gambling addict and lost his tuition money. He gambled it back along with about $1,000 extra that he sent to his family. He never gambled again, stating that when he won back his tuition money he had "conquered my passion right then and there."

Since Tesla finished his studies so quickly, he had several weeks (sometimes months) between semesters where he was free to wander the Gračac forests, teaching himself English by reading books by Charles Dickens and Mark Twain.

When his third year of schooling began, Tesla was nowhere to be found. He was living in a cave, conducting more electro-mechanical experiments made out of scrap metal and salvaged glass. By the time he arrived at school, the semester was almost over. Tesla asked for an extension on his final exam so that he could have a few days to study for it. His request was denied, and Tesla dropped out of college.

He avoided his family as much as possible in order to keep his dropping out of school a secret. He started a rumor that he had drowned in the Mur River, and his friends and family thought him dead. He worked as a draftsman during this period, and eventually suffered a nervous breakdown.

He continued working in Prague as a draftsman, then later in Budapest, where he created a telephone amplifier for the hard of hearing. It was never patented or sold commercially. But word of the invention reached France, where the Con Edison company invited him to come work for them. The chief engineers there were impressed enough with his work to send him to Menlo Park to work directly with Thomas Edison, with whom he had been corresponding with on the subject of direct current generators. He arrived in the US with four cents in his pocket and a letter of recommendation to Edison from his French boss that read "I know two great men and you are one of them; the other is this young man."

Edison was impressed with the young Tesla and put him to work designing direct current generators. Tesla told Edison that he could completely redesign each generator so that productivity and efficiency would be doubled, if not tripled. "There's fifty thousand dollars in it for you—if you can do it," Edison told Tesla.

After six months, Tesla accomplished the feat. He went to Edison to inquire about the $50,000, and was quickly dismissed by his boss. "You don't understand American humor," Edison said. Edison then offered to give Tesla a $10.00 a week raise in recognition for his work. Tesla spit on the floor and walked out of the Menlo Park compound for good.

## THE WAR OF THE CURRENTS

Tesla had been experimenting with Alternating Current, which was superior in every way to Direct Current. While Edison was busy trying to convert New York to the less efficient and more dangerous Direct Current, Tesla was wowing financial backers by the seemingly limitless superiority of Alternating Current.

Unlike DC, AC power didn't need a substation set up every few hundred yards to maintain the flow of electricity; AC could be generated for miles on a single line. Unlike DC, AC was "self regulated" in the amount of voltage it put out. (Several of the early houses equipped with Edison's Direct Current burned down as a result of an electrical fire caused by the inherent limitations of DC power.)

Tesla started his own company, Tesla Electric Light and Manufacturing, which sought to provide Alternating Current to thousands of homes all around the world. But Edison was busy working on a smear campaign that painted Tesla as a madman and AC power as hazardous and unpredictable. Edison used his motion picture company to film the electrocution of Topsy, the tortured elephant (*see STE Volume One*) which was done using AC power. Edison scared the public by saying "would you allow an electrical flow into your home that was so strong that it could electrocute an elephant?" (Edison failed to mention that the elephant could have been electrocuted using a third of the voltage of his own DC power.)

The propaganda scared Tesla's backers into withdrawing their cash. Penniless once again, Tesla went to work digging ditches for the next couple of years. Eventually, with the help of George Westinghouse, he rebuilt his company and began the hard sell of touting AC electricity as the wave of the future.

At the 1893 World's Fair in Chicago, Tesla shocked audiences by making his body an electrical outlet. By touching a generator, Tesla shot sparks from his hand and powered electrical devices merely by pointing at them. He explained that the amount of current running through his body was quite safe, as it avoided the vital organs and exited throughout his arm. "The same amount of voltage, if it were DC power, would have killed me instantly," he explained to the crowd.

Public favor soon turned towards AC power. Edison's lies and misrepresentations were swept under the rug as he conceded to Tesla's superior current, and all of Edison's DC machinery was converted to AC. By the time the "War of the Currents" was over, both J.P. Morgan (Edison's financial backer) and George Westinghouse (Tesla's backer) were nearly broke. Morgan was nearly bankrupt from the demise of DC electricity, and he refused to loan any more money to Westinghouse, who was in deep debt from the building of early AC lines and power stations, of which he had not seen a return on yet. Westinghouse cut ties with Tesla after purchasing all of the patents for Alternating Current technology for 216,000 dollars.

# Thomas, Tesla and Tobacco

When Nikola Tesla first arrived on US shores, he went through great lengths to appear as though he was an European aristocrat. He carried a pearled snuff box with the picture of his mother inlaid within the lid, and offered it around to the company at hand, as was the custom of the era.

What many people didn't know was that socially, Tesla was a complete fraud. He was too poor to afford the expensive tailored suits that he wore, so he worked with a funeral director manufacturing embalming fluid for corpses. The funeral director paid Tesla off by giving him the expensive suits that rich men had recently been buried in, or were scheduled to be cremated in. Thus, Nikola Tesla always appeared dapper and dashing, even when he was at his lowest point in life, digging ditches and graves for 2 dollars a week.

Though he once wrote of snuff as being a "mystical elixir" that cleared his head and allowed him to concentrate tightly on complex theorems, he more often referred to tobacco as "a poison." More specifically, he meant smoking. Tesla could not stand to be near someone smoking a pipe or cigar (although he seemed not to harbor any grudge towards cigarette smokers) and he positively detested tobacco chewers, who he (correctly) attributed the epidemical outbreak of tuberculoses to.

It is not known how often, or how much, Tesla's use of snuff was a genuine passion or part of his "Wealthy Socialite" alter ego. In his private writings, he only mentioned snuff twice, both times favorably.

If the $50,000 renege from Thomas Edison wasn't enough to cause Tesla to hate the man, then surely his smoking habit was enough to drive the young Serb mad. Edison habitually puffed on long Havana cigars. They were said to "stink to high heaven" by those close to him. At home he often smoked a long Churchwarden pipe. The length of the pipe probably made it impractical to smoke at work, where Edison needed his hands free. Edison also chewed plug tobacco and kept several cast iron cuspidors throughout the premises. He snuffed socially, but was not a heavy snuffer by any means.

Something that Edison did not tolerate in the slightest was cigarettes and cigarette smokers. He believed that cigarettes were poisonous, and that they made smokers feeble in strength and mental capacity. Automobile innovator Henry Ford hated cigarettes with a passion, and wrote an anti-cigarette tract called "The Little White Slaver," which Edison enjoyed most thoroughly. He wrote back to Henry Ford after reading his pamphlet:

*Friend Ford,*

*The injurious agent in cigarettes comes principally from the burning paper wrapper. The substance thereby formed, is called "Acrolein." It has a violent action on the nerve centers, producing degeneration of the cells of the brain, which is quite rapid among boys.*

*Unlike most narcotics this degeneration is permanent and uncontrollable. I employ no person who smokes cigarettes.*

*Your friend,*
*Thos. A. Edison*

Of course, there wasn't (and never has been) a substance like the so-called "Acrolein" present in cigarette smoke, but between the efforts of men like Edison, Ford and Charles Lindbergh (who never smoked or drank, but used approximately 100 grams of snus a day) the cigarette temperance movement gained professional credence from some of the most respected innovators of the era. The movement became sidelined by alcohol prohibition, but picked right up after the repealing of the 18th Amendment.

STE

# TESLA'S DEATH RAY

One of the most enigmatic of all of Tesla's projects is his so-called "death ray," a device that was capable of destroying life in heretofore unthinkable volumes.

Tesla's Ray was in theory the ultimate peace keeping device. He had built a tower that sent an almost limitless amount of currency towards a directed target, destroying it upon contact.

Tesla understood the inherent danger of any country having such a powerful device, and he created many failsafes that would keep the ray from attacking other countries; it would only function as a defensive device within the borders of one's own country.

When word of his weapon circulated among world leaders, they demanded a working prototype, or at least the blueprints that showed the device was functional. So that no one country had an advantage against the other, Tesla divvied up the blueprints between countries, with Austria, Spain, Sweden, Great Britain, Germany and the US each receiving part of the plans. They were useless by themselves, but when combined, they proved that a death ray was both possible and easy to mass-produce.

But Tesla had great reservations about creating machinery that could kill millions on contact. Before he could deliver the final blueprint for the apparatus that made the death ray operational, he suddenly had a change of heart and withdrew all plans from the hands of the countries that previously showed interest in the "superdefense system". Tesla would later burn his plans, declaring that he would rather save lives instead of destroying them.

The press labeled Tesla a "kook" and pretty soon all of the "mad scientist" types portrayed in B-Movies and comic books bore a striking similarity to Nikola Tesla. His work was called 'drivel' by fellow scientists and was soon forgotten by the public at large.

While Tesla's Death Ray never saw the light of day, Reagan's "Star Wars" program was designed around it. Another daily reminder of the feasibility of Tesla's death ray towers is used by almost every developed nation on Earth: the Cellular Phone towers that dot our landscape are built almost exactly to Tesla's original defense tower specifications.

# TESLA READY FOR BUSINESS.

## HE HAS BOUGHT THE LAND FOR HIS WIRELESS TELEGRAPHY STATION AND LET THE CONTRACTS FOR THE BUILDINGS.

Nikola Tesla's plans for a transatlantic wireless telegraphic system are now so well in hand that he has bought a site for the station on the Long Island shore, and has agents looking for a suitable place for a station on the British coast. The station in this country will be at Wardenclyffe, on the Sound, nine miles east of Port Jefferson. Mr. Tesla has purchased two hundred acres of land in that vicinity, and closed contracts yesterday for the necessary buildings.

Five or six buildings will be erected on different parts of the tract, the largest of which is to be one hundred feet square and several stories high. It will contain, Mr. Tesla says, one of the most complete electrical plants that can be purchased. Three hundred and fifty horsepower will be developed, and the total cost will be nearly $150,000. The other buildings will be used for the electrical experiments with which Mr. Tesla is now engaged, including a system of lighting by diffused light. He will probably give up his present laboratory, at No. 46 East Houston-st., and make his headquarters at Wardenclyffe.

Mr. Tesla has been working for several years with his system of wireless telegraphy, and believes that he has advanced far enough to warrant a change from the experimental to the commercial stage. He says it will not be long before he will be transmitting commercial messages between Wardenclyffe and Europe without the use of wires or cables.

When seen at the Waldorf-Astoria Hotel last night Mr. Tesla said:

"I would have been sending messages across the ocean without the use of wires by this time if the public were not so hard to convince that it could be done. It takes time to assure people of the truth of new discoveries. It was six or eight years before people believed in my system of transmitting electric power. Now it is used everywhere. I cannot tell you just how far I have advanced in the perfection of my system of telegraphy, but I hope soon to be able to show most convincing results."

# TESLA'S "POST WAR" RESEARCH

With the money that Tesla received from his sales to Westinghouse, he was free to experiment on things that he had waited years to begin on. Wardenclyffe Tower, also known as the Tesla Tower, was a huge wireless transmission center that pre-dated the internet by some 55 years. Had the tower been completed, fax machines, email broadcasters, cellular phones, wi-fi transmissions, high definition television and radio signals, and intergalactic communication would have been capable under Tesla's designs.

For funding, Tesla went to JP Morgan, the banker who used to finance Edison and was painfully aware that he had initially put his eggs in the wrong basket now that the world was running on AC energy. But when Tesla started talking about making all of these innovations available to the public *for free*, Morgan got cold feet and pulled out from the project. He decided he'd rather rake in the royalties from the existing power stations and lines he already owned. In doing so, the world of technology was set back at least sixty years.

Eventually, the Wardenclyffe deed was turned over from Tesla to George Boldt, proprietor of the Waldorf-Astoria, to pay a $20,000 debt (about $400,000 today). In 1917, around the time that the Wardenclyffe Tower was demolished by Boldt to make the land a more viable real estate asset, Tesla ironically received the AIEE's highest honor, the Edison Medal. Tesla would end up puttering himself into poverty, his last major patent being for an early version of the helicopter. Though he continued to invent and experiment up to his death in 1943, he died deeply in debt on January 7th in Room 3327 of the New Yorker Hotel. He was cremated as a pauper and for many years his cremains were unaccounted for. Eventually they were located and are now stored at the Nikola Tesla Museum in Belgrade.

Tesla outlived his arch-rival Edison by 12 years. Both men made almost unfathomable leaps forward in technology, but it has always been Edison that received the lion's share of the credit. With the advent of the internet (itself partially birthed by the "Mad Serbian") is finally beginning to be recognized for his work in science, and it's an accepted fact in the scientific community that Tesla did more to advance the progress of the world than Edison ever could have accomplished without his "worker elves" at Menlo Park.

Let us remember these two men, the next time we turn on a lightswitch, watch our televisions, log into our cellphones and computers, or play back music on any form of radio, MP3 or CD device.

Finally, let's remember these men each time we take a pinch of snuff, and ponder how much these men would have accomplished *without* the help of tobacco.

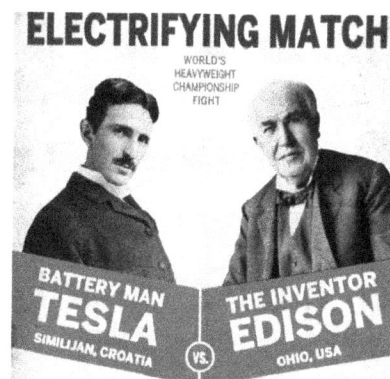

**ELECTRIFYING MATCH**

WORLD'S HEAVYWEIGHT CHAMPIONSHIP FIGHT

BATTERY MAN **TESLA** SIMILIJAN, CROATIA · VS. · THE INVENTOR **EDISON** OHIO, USA

STE

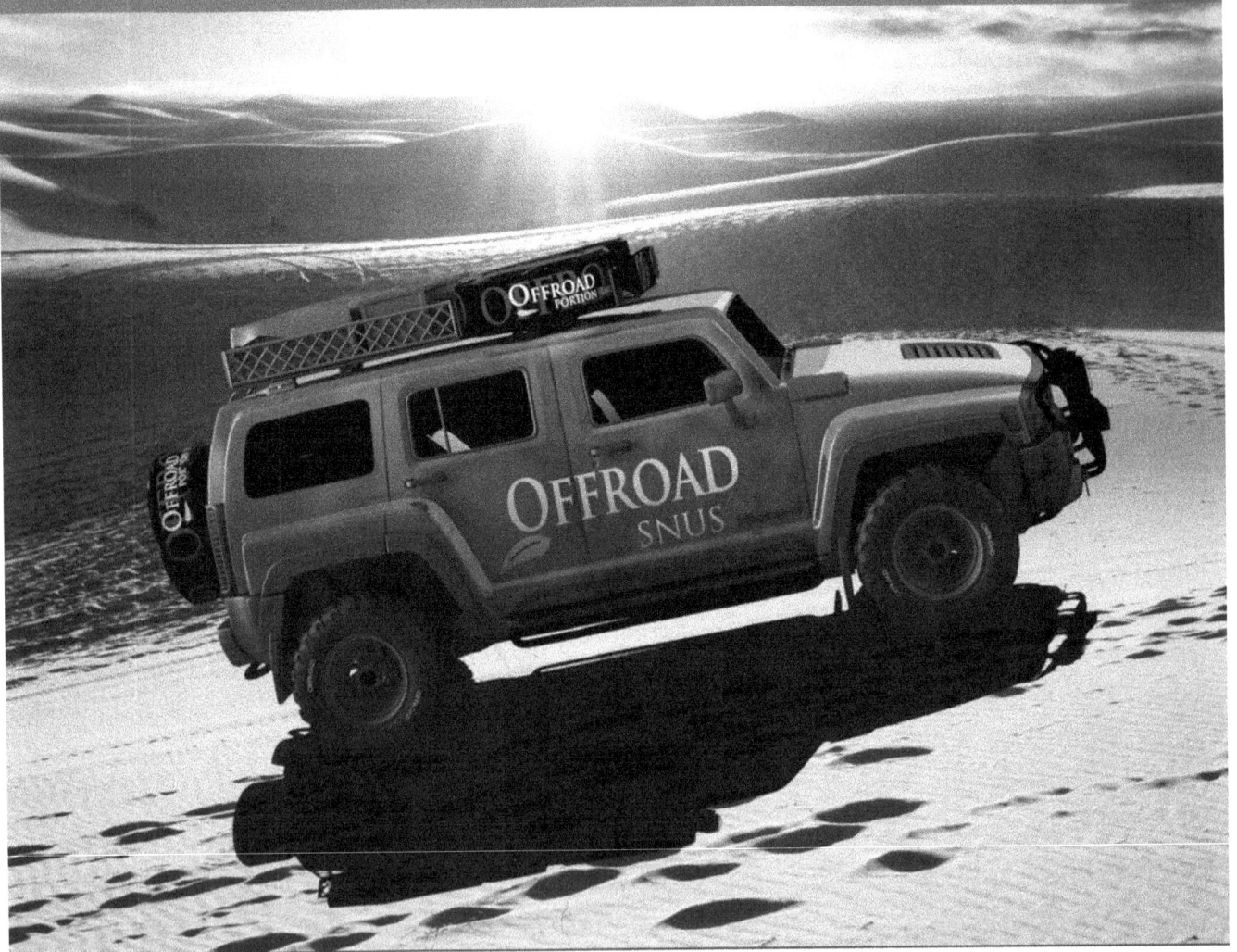

# OFFROAD
## SNUS

WARNING: This product is not a safe alternative to cigarettes

# Snus King:

## Ljunglöf's *Ettan* And The History Of Swedish Snus

## An Ephemeris Exclusive

Original text by the Swedish Tobacco Museum

## CHAPTER SIX:

## THE EMPIRE GROWS

The mass emigration moved a quarter of Sweden's population to the US. Ljunglöf was intrigued by this new market, but he had one obstacle blocking his path: The Atlantic Ocean.

The Swedes that left the rock mines and Luther's Catechism for a better life in the new country mainly settled in the Northeast, and most of those immigrants did indeed find the better life that they had hoped for. Work was abundant, and the class segregation so rigorously structured in Sweden was not to be found in America. But most of the immigrants still felt the occasional homesickness for their mother land, and this longing was felt even worse by snusers.

With each new boat dropping off fresh immigrants, desperate letters addressed to "loving brothers" and "caring sisters" implored them to send back some snus to America. One of these sisters brought along with her a keg of snus covered by a shawl, in order to escape the prying eyes of customs agents at the Canadian border. (Even 130 years ago, Canada taxed tobacco outrageously.) By the time she made it to Hill Top, Winnipeg, she had collapsed on the road under the weight of the snus barrel. Her grandson rolled the keg the rest of the way.

More entrepreneurial-minded emigrants had ideas of starting their own snus factories. After all, American was tobacco country. Snuff mills were soon overrun by Swedish workers, eager to get to cooking. The Main Streets in Swedish neighborhoods in Chicago, Minneapolis and New York were all known as "Snus Boulevard." Many American snuff mills tried to make snus that fit the tastes of Swedish snusers, even describing it as "Original Swedish Snus straight from the Old Country," but it just wasn't the same, and it definitely couldn't hold a candle to Ljunglöf's Ettan. The emigrant's frustration could be summed up in the following dispatch to the Göteborg Post:

NEXT PAGE: THE LJUNGLÖF LIVING ROOM

# The Shipping Problem

*"Good snus can't be bought for love or for money."*

The problems with shipping snus over the Atlantic were numerous. Aside from the expected shipping delays, rotten snus and pirated cargo, there was the everyday problem of missing shipments and slow (or no) communication overseas. One letter from New York snus retailer J. Påhlsson to Swedish wholesalers Larsson Brothers & Co. illustrates this frustration:

*To H. Herrar, Larsson Brothers & Co.*
*Malmo*

...In regards to my repeated inquiries as to where my keg of snus is, the only answer I can hope to expect from you is nothing. ... I fully expect to die of old age before I receive an answer to this correspondence.

J. Påhlsson
c/o Mr. J. Nilsson
No. 688 5th Avenue, Newyork city
Nord Amerika

But help for emigrants was on the way. Ljunglöf began wrapping the snus containers in tinfoil, which at that time was an expensive commodity in Sweden. It kept his snus fresh during shipment and it also markedly distanced himself from his competitors in the lengths that he would go through to keep his Ettan the best snus in the world, even as far away as Chicago and Alaska.

Speaking of worldwide distribution, Ljunglöf's most famous customer soon surfaced, this time in the far off city-state of the Vatican, where his snus found favor with God's chosen representative on earth, Pope Leo XIII.

Known as the "people's pope", Leo kept a close ear to the ground in order to find out what was popular in the secular world. To find favor with the masses, he would often follow whatever trends appealed to the lower and middle classes. When snuff use became an activity that was almost universally practiced, Leo put out a call for his staff to bring him snuff from all over the world. He would then pick the blend that suited him best.

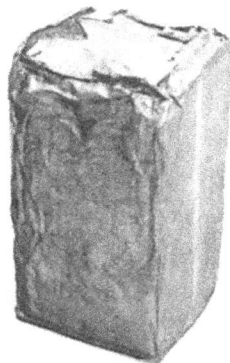

**Left:** Knut Ljunglöf's innovative thinking led to the use of lead or zinc tin foil wrapped around snus packages. Several layers were applied in order to keep the snus as fresh as possible during the long journey across the Atlantic Ocean.

**Right:** Pope Leo XIII during a procession. Notice the two Cardinals in front grasping Swedish-style brass snuff boxes, most likely containing Ettan.

Luckily for the Pope, he had a Swedish Chamberlain named Claes Lagergren who just happened to use Ettan.

Papal custom dictated that the snuffbox was passed from Chamberlain to Cardinal, who would then open the snuffbox, take a pinch, and present it to the Pope. (The idea was to keep the Pope's white robe from becoming soiled.) When Lagergren handed over the Ettan to the Cardinal, the nervous young man spilled the entire contents of the snuff box all over the Pope's gleaming white robe!

Instead of becoming angry, Leo scraped the moist snuff off of his robe and put it in his mouth. The entire room held its breath. After a few seconds, a broad smile spread over the Pope's face and the congregation breathed a sigh of relief. He immediately ordered Chamberlain Lagergren to put in an order to the Ljunglöf factory in Stockholm. The Snuff King's popularity continued to grow, as well as his wealth.

## THE NEW ESTATE

The Summer House in Canaan was becoming too small for a man in Knut Ljunglöf's position. Construction on the "Big House" began in 1893 near Blackeburg, just south of the old residence. The new house was in all reality a castle, surrounded by rare trees such as silver fir, cypress, copper beech and Chinese apple. Palm trees and agaves grew during the summer.

The home was officially opened on Knut Ljunglöf's 60th birthday amid much pomp and circumstance. The castle and its surroundings were a stunning testament to the Snus King's success. Those invited to the party included the cream of Stockholm's merchant class. Even King Oscar II made an appearance.

It was sort of an informal state visit whenever the King of Sweden visited Knut's residences. If Dröttningholm was the "little Versailles," Blackeberg was Dröttningholm in miniature.

After a great meal, socialites would walk out on gravel paths, towards Mälaren beach and up to the tower to take their punch. From there it was a breathtaking view over the water and bathhouse (with integrated basin) as well as the bridge with the two steam yachts *Anna* and *Tullia*, the latter named after Knut's mother.

RIGHT:

KNUT LJUNGLÖF'S SECOND WIFE, HULDA LJUNGLÖF (NÉE BROMAN.)

The tower was the height of excitement on the grounds, especially for the kids at Blackeberg, but it lost its charm and became downright eerie once it became the family tomb for deceased Ljunglöf relatives.

Ljunglöf, over time, became to be regarded as a "flashy" type of socialite, in star contrast to his father. This "playboy" type of lifestyle caused his first marriage to dissolve and his wife took custody of the four children. Ljunglöf quickly remarried the widow of a young officer.

*Background: Hundreds of Swedish Emigrants board a Göteborg steamer heading for New York.*

ABOVE: DALKULLAN SWEDISH IMPORT SHOP, NEW YORK, 1888. THE MOST IN-DEMAND IMPORT FROM SWEDEN WAS ALWAYS SNUS (PARTICULARLY LJUNGLÖF'S), AND MANY SHOPS SPRANG UP TO OFFER IT, LIKE THE CANADIAN SHOP ADVERTISING **BELOW**. THE DALKULLAN SHOP WAS NOTABLE FOR ALSO OFFERING ITS OWN BLEND OF SNUS, ADVERTISED **LEFT** AND **RIGHT**.

## Svenskt Snus

Stockholm (Ljunglöfs) och Swedish Rappe, $1.25 pr. pound. Sändes mot förskottsbetalning af $1.25.

## ERZINGERS

McINTYRE BLOCK, WINNIPEG

ABOVE: THE "BIG HOUSE" DURING IT'S HEYDAY, CA. 1900.

LEFT: LJUNGLÖF WITH HIS PRIZED HUNTING DOGS.

BELOW: THE LJUNGLÖF BANQUET HALL.

Captain Axel Broman was a friend of Ljunglöf who rented a summer home on one of Knut's estates, Little Ängby. The two were close for many years and usually took a walk together at night through the garden.

Broman ended up taking ill, and on his deathbed, he placed his wife Hulda's hand in Ljunglöf's, and nodded his approval. The two were soon married and the relationship brought Knut three stepdaughters. (Many of the Ljunglöf's associates thought that the oldest girl was actually Knut's biological child. It was common knowledge among the Ljunglöf family that Knut and Hulda carried on a long term affair behind their spouse's backs, although it was a subject never spoken of. Though Knut's wife was aware of the affair, it is unclear if Axel Broman ever knew of the secret relationship). The new marriage soon produced a son, Robert Ljunglöf.

## THE WILDLIFE

"Mother Nature in a luxury package." These were the words used by Knut to describe the grounds of the Ljunglöf estate. (Townspeople had another, less eloquent moniker for it: "the rich man's dream.") A team of horses and a fleet of yachts were kept at the ready, all hours of the day, in case Knut decided to make use of them.

Knut's most prized possession, however, was his magnificent team of thoroughbred hunting dogs, which was worth the equivalent of about one million US dollars in today's currency. He put his long-time assistant Johan Andersson in charge of one task only- care and feeding of the hounds. Though he would visit the dogs every afternoon, Knut made sure to call the gamekeeper every night before bedtime to make sure that the dogs were alright. Andersson's daughter, Tora, recalled the nightly phone calls:

Every night the phone would ring. My father would answer, and we would overhear the conversation. "Good evening. Yes, we're fine, thank you. Yes, the dogs are fine. Yes, they've been fed and watered. Yes, they all feel good. Thank you. Good evening, Mr. Ljunglöf."

## DIGNIFIED PUNCTUALITY

Knut began rearing his son to command the family business almost from birth. He expanded the staff of his home to include maids, doctors and teachers that were always on hand for the sake of the children, especially his son Robert. Knut placed great emphasis on the education of his children.

Knut himself was the epitome of professionalism in all aspects of his home life. He would wait for everyone at the table to take their seat before taking his, and his mannerisms were slight and dignified. Even his snus use was refined, never placing any of it in his mouth while women were present, and most certainly not while in conversation with company. He would politely excuse himself and come back with a small amount of Ettan tucked under his lip, barely detectable to his guests.

With the same punctual dedication, he inspected his snus factory every day, verifying the temperature in his sweating room and sampling the days product before it shipped out, just as his father did before him. He would walk from one end of the factory to the other, his hands firmly clasped behind his back. He inspected the machinery and would even stop to sweep up a spill on the floor if no one else was around to do it.

Ljunglöf demanded the same level of perfection out of his workers. He wanted the factory to be spotless, and all mechanical parts to be cleaned and wiped down at the end of the day. His worker's outfits were tailor-made and spotless; they were cleaned by the factory's own laundry system. Knut demanded that the floor should always be clean enough "to eat off of." And it was.

Ljunglöf ran his factory like a true patriarch. The employees had work and a pension for old age, and a decent retirement package, which were rare luxuries in that day. The workers were also entitled to a large parcel of Ettan to take home everyday, enough to share with even their friends and family.

"Papa Knut" felt sore even for the elders in the city. At the front of the workhouse every day, the elderly could pack snus in their boxes at the factory. The idea was good, but it was soon derailed when the line outside the factory got longer, and the containers got bigger and bigger.

Finally Ljunglöf decided to supply free snus in kegs directly to the poorhouses.

## FREE SNUS FOR ALL!

Though he could be quite miserly with his money, Knut was vain when it came to his snus, and he allowed his workers to take home one parcel a day, enough for not only the worker, but his friends and family as well. Eventually this lead to an overzealous consumption of Ettan, along with black market sales from company workers.

In 1901, Knut eventually put his foot down and did away with the free snus program. The next day, an angry, but carefully worded petition with 53 signatures came back from the factory workers imploring Mr. Ljunglof to "not let just a few bad apples spoil the entire bunch." They begged him to reinstate the free snus program, as the potential for theft would be too strong for "weak minded" workers.

Ljunglof's response was thus: "In careful overview of the situation, we admit that every one of our workers in the packing room are entitled to a quantum of snus, which he will agree to use only for his own consumption." And so the crisis was avoided.

LJUNGLÖF FAMILY PORTRAIT, 1905

With the new century beginning, Knut found himself slowing down. He didn't have the same enthusiasm for snus making that his father possessed at the same age.

Though he was losing interest in his empire, his passion for quality still remained. But he knew it was time to pass the throne on to Robert.

Though Knut was too frail for hunting, he still loved his dogs dearly and turned them over to his son. Robert had inherited his love of sport from his father and grandfather. He also started a sanctuary for wounded animals, even constructing a bird hospital to nurse crows with broken wings back to health.

The larger yacht *Tullia* took the family a couple of times a year to Gålö or Skå Edeby, fully staffed with a Captain, engineer, butler and cook. The Captain's main task throughout the year was to hoist and haul flags at Ljunglöfs castle.

Gasoline-powered automobiles soon entered the country and city. Ljunglöf's modern factory was quickly outfitted with small trucks, and Ljunglöf himself imported a luxury sedan, complete with private chauffeur, hardly an unexpected purchase for one of the country's richest men.

Knut himself never cared to learn how to drive, he loved to ride. His chauffeur, Bergman, was famous for the speed and grace in which he would zip along the hills and narrow roadways of Blackeburg.

LEFT: ROBERT LJUNGLÖF, 1908.

# THE WOODEN LEG

Knut still continued his daily walks. When walking in the city, he would have one of his staff accompany him and check on the affairs at the factory. Alone, he would walk the gardens of his estate.

Ljunglöf developed an infection in one of his legs, and his stubbornness in seeing a doctor resulted in the wound becoming gangrenous. Still refusing medical aid, the gangrene spread from his knee to his foot; the skin was so badly decayed that his bones were visible.

His family begged him to see a doctor, but Ljunglöf refused. He had a phobia about hospitals and bluntly stated that he would rather die than check into one. The family made hasty arrangements for a team of physicians to come to the estate. White sheets were hung from wall to wall and a makeshift hospice was created in Knut's bedroom.

When the head physician pulled back the sheet covering Knut's leg, he almost vomited. Maggots had begun to fester in the rotten leg and the stench was overpowering. The prognosis was short and direct: the leg would have to be amputated. Knut readily agreed, but refused to go to the hospital in order to have the procedure done. The doctors begged him to come to the hospital to have the operation, where all the necessary equipment was at hand and the conditions were sanitary. "If I can't find an old sawbones to take it off right here in my own bed, then I'll just let it fester until I die. Mohammed couldn't get to the mountain, and so the mountain came to Mohammed." As usual, Knut got his way.

The dining hall was cordoned off and the entire room was sanitized from floor to ceiling with boiling water. Knut was lifted onto the heavy wooden table and tied down with rope. He was given ether as an anaesthetic. A small block of wood wrapped with twine was placed in his mouth for him to bite down on, but he spat it out. "Give me some goddamned snus instead, if you want me to keep my mouth shut." A bowl of Ettan was promptly brought to Knut and a sizeable prilla was placed in his mouth. A team of surgeons from Sabbatsberg Hospital was brought in and went to work immediately.

For antiseptic and disinfectant purposes, Carbolic Acid was used, which Knut half-consciously recognized by its unique scent. (It is unclear whether or not he dreamed of sterilized cattle cars, spoiled Ettan, and angry customer complaints while under sedation...)

The amputation was a success, and fortunately the gangrene had not spread any further. When he awoke from his short coma, Knut was, as usual, all business. "Where in the hell is my new leg?"

"You'll want to give your leg time to heal before we affix a wooden peg to it," explained the doctor. "It could get infected otherwise."

"Well," answered Knut sarcastically, "if this new leg gets gangrene I'll be sure and whittle away the bad parts." That evening, he was up and about, walking around with his new wooden prosthesis.

The amputation was kept secret from everyone outside of the family. After the surgery, Knut actually seemed to be happier than he had been in years. "I'm finally the pirate I've always wanted to be since childhood," he would say, pointing to his peg leg. With his plain grey suit, his white, bushy muttonchop sideburns, bulbous red nose, ever-present bandanna wrapped around his neck, and his Captain's hat (awarded to him by the Royal Swedish Yacht Club), he looked every bit the salty sea captain who had spent most of his life sailing the world. He would even occasionally don an eye-patch and lovingly chase his grandchildren around the yard, pretending to be the ghost of Davy Jones or Blackbeard the Pirate.

## THE TWILIGHT YEARS

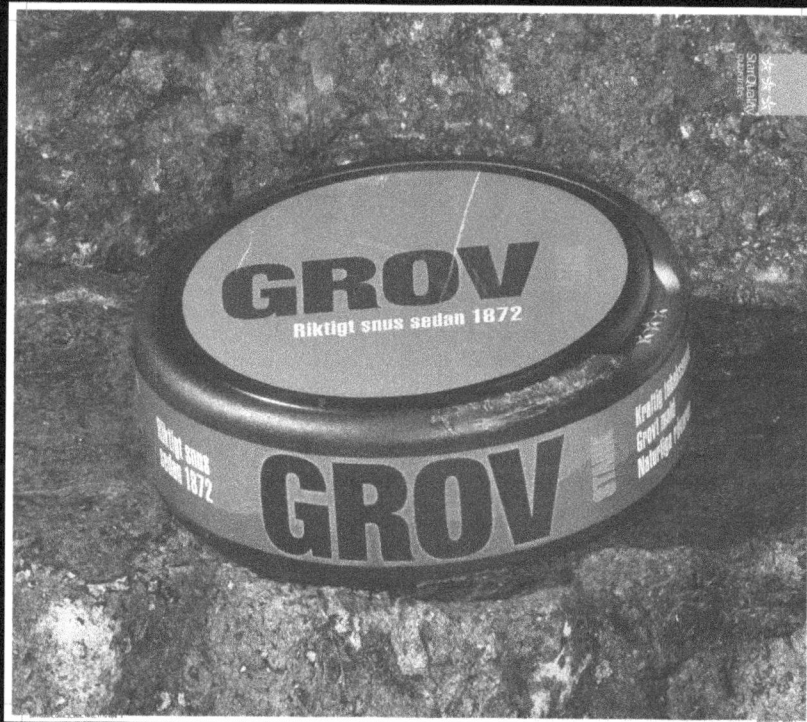

Q: What's New From

★★★
**SWEDISH MATCH** ?

WARNING: This product can cause mouth cancer.

# A: Everything.

New flavors. Expanded Distribution. Improved pouch material. New can designs. All at the same reasonable price you've come to expect from the world's greatest snus maker.

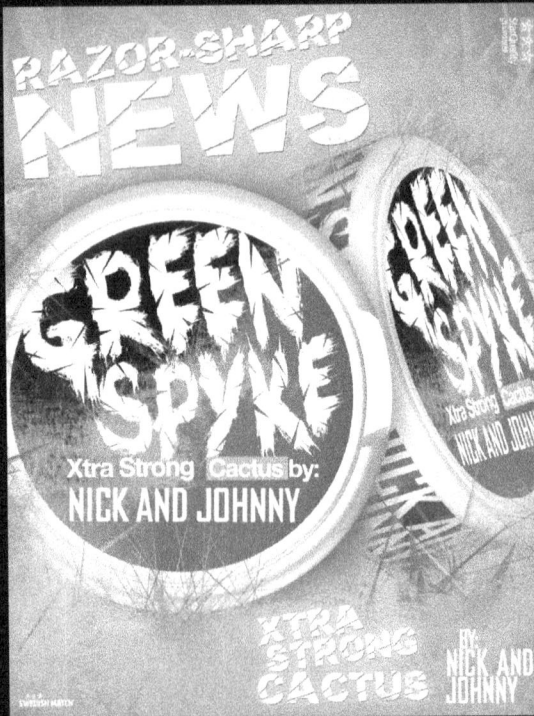

Available now from Snuscentral.Com and other fine tobacconists worldwide.

Most of Knut Ljunglöf's close friends had long since passed away. The famous opera singer Jenny Lind and the social activist Fredrika Bremer were gone, and the former King Oscar II lived a secluded, broken existence after the union between Norway and Sweden crumbled away.

Ljunglöf soon found himself sliding back into his crabby old self, disgusted with the new crop of *nouveau riche* upstarts that reveled in their wealth by wrecking expensive sports cars and sinking priceless yachts all for the "fun of it." It was quite clear that they had never had to work for their money, and that they had no respect for cash. This new wave of Swedish socialite made Knut bitter and spiteful.

Determined to not let his son become part of this disturbing scene, he sent Robert to military school, which he attended between 1900 to 1908. (It was rumored that Robert was sent to military school primarily because his father thought him to possibly be homosexual. Stories circulated about Robert cavorting romantically with a male school friend. Knut thought that a strict disciplinary environment would "cure" Robert of his sexual orientation. Though Robert would later marry twice in his life, neither relationship produced an heir to the Ljunglöf throne.)

With Robert away at military school, Knut turned his attention to his stepdaughters. He hoped to marry them off soon, and gently nudged them towards finding a suitor.

**********

Growing up in one of Stockholm's richest families and inheriting their mother's good looks, many boys were interested in courting 17 year old Maria (called "Mille") and 19 year old Elsa. Elsa, the flamboyant redhead, was the exact opposite of quiet and reserved Mille, who seemed to show no interest in boys.

Elsa danced at Amaranten and Innocencen, sat in the JF Ljunglöf box at the Stockholm Opera House and flirted with handsome officers. Elsa soon fell in love with a young lieutenant, Malcolm Warner Holms. The two were quickly married in a lavish ceremony.

Though Holms was madly in love with Elsa, she soon had regrets after the ceremony, believing that she had "married poor." The Holms' inherited the old "Small House" and produced one son, Eric. He described his formative years in the book *Diligence and Flair:*

ELSA (ABOVE) AND MILLE (RIGHT) LJUNGLOF.

*"Dad was a poor soldier, and felt like such. They received an annual stipend from [Knut] and lived like peasants within a mansion. Mother toiled like a servant maid in silent protest of her unextravagant home life."*

Sven Hedin was another suitor to the Ljunglöf household, this time to Mille. Hedin wasn't a millionaire, but he was a well known and famous world explorer and adventurer. Hedin loved Mille with an intense, burning love that was not apparently reciprocated by the young lady. In one of the diaries he kept during his voyages to Tibet in 1896, he wrote:

*"It was a black day today, when the courier arrived. One of the letters mentioned a rumor that the love of my life was about to be engaged to another man. My eyes were blackened, for I could not think of a life without her. It was for her sake that I conquered the heart of Asia, Tibet and the Gobi Desert."*

A few years later, they met again, and Hedin was elated to learn that the engagement had been broken off. He proposed marriage to her on the spot.

Mille told Sven that she would marry him on one condition: that he abandon his wanderings and settle down with her. Hedin agreed, but at the last minute, he broke off the engagement. He knew that eventually his wanderlust would return and he would have no control over it. He pledged his undying love to her and wished her the best luck in life, and returned to Tibet.

Mille later married another man. Hedin bitterly replied upon hearing the news that "Asia is now my mistress." Yet on his deathbed, decades later, he passed away clutching a photograph of his beloved Mille.     STE

*Next issue: our eighth (and final) chapter of the Ljunglöf saga. The Swedish government steps in and takes control of all tobacco production, effectively ending the reign the of the Ljunglof snus dynasty. Don't miss it!*

# TOBACCO

## AND ITS——

# BONDAGE.

——BY A——

## Slave Who Became Free.

### LESTER C. HUBBARD.

PRICE, 25 CENTS.

LIBERATOR PUBLISHING CO.
BOSTON, 1898.

# FOREWORD

## BY
## RW HUBBARD

As an amateur genealogist, I was pretty surprised when I learned that about 85% of all Hubbards in America were descended from two English cousins that settled in Connecticut and Boston, respectively. What surprised me even more was how many of my ancestors were writers, publishers, or poets. There's Gardiner Greene Hubbard, who started up *National Geographic,* still in publication to this day.

Elbert Hubbard, was a social anarchist (dubbed "the first hippie") who died aboard the *RMS Lusitania* 1915. Elbert was a self publisher who ran afoul of the US Postal Service for sending out a book that claimed "Jesus was an Anarchist" and was jailed for sending out "objectionable" material thru the postal system. (His fine and his criminal record were erased by his cousin, another of my ancestors, politician William Jennings Bryan).

Then there's L. Ron Hubbard. Let me make this distinction once and for all for every reader that writes in to ask me whether I'm related to him or (even worse) if I'm a practicing scientologist. L. Ron Hubbard is/was of no blood relation to any other Hubbard on this planet. His father was an orphan named Henry August Wilson who was taken in by a family named Hubbard, and so adopted their surname. (So there. The pedophilic pulp sci-fi author is not my grandfather, as has been erroneously reported.)

But every so often I come across a work by someone bearing the Hubbard surname. One such book, *Tobacco and Its Bondage*, was written by a Lester C. Hubbard out of Boston, Mass. I checked my familial charts and sure enough, he was a distant relative of mine. In fact, during the Civil War, he fought (for the Union) at the Capture of New Orleans against my great-great-great Grandfather, who fought for the Confederacy. They were eighth cousins. (The war may not have been "brother against brother" as it's so often portrayed, but in my family it was definitely "cousin against cousin" in numerous circumstances.)

Anyway, getting back to the book. It's typical of many of the anti-tobacco tracts of the day. While not as sensational as Crane's *Assassin of Liberty* or as self-indulgent as King James' *Counterblaste*, it's still an interesting, unintentionally humorous account of one man's struggle with cigar addiction. I humbly present my ancestor's unedited and unvarnished tract denouncing "that demon nicotine" within a forum that I'm sure will have him turning in his grave.

Top to bottom:
Elbert Hubbard (eccentric essayist),
Gardiner Greene Hubbard (founder of *National Geographic*,)
L. Ron Hubbard (Satan Incarnate)

In consequence-of the peculiar manner in which I took it up and left it off, I know more about the tobacco habit, through personal experience, than any other man I ever heard of. This is not said in vanity, but that my story may receive the consideration I believe it merits.

Most men slip gradually into this addiction while in their teens, whereas I did not fall under the indulgence until after I became a captain in the army during our great war. I had no sooner commenced, however, than I used tobacco excessively, hence its evil effects soon followed. Not that I observed them at the time, because, like all other fresh victims, I was blind to the facts in my own case.

But now that I am emancipated, all the incidents of my long serfdom stand out with startling clearness, and I see that in one short year after forming the habit degeneracy in character began. I lost ambition, ideality and high moral purpose, becoming almost the reverse of what I had been twelve months before.

While so sharp an accentuation of the baneful results of tobacco is rarely met with, it none the less truly reveals the actual nature of the blighting curse and shows what it is doing to a greater or less extent in the case of every young man using it.

After a slavery of nearly a third of a century, I broke my bonds. If I had become free by reason of any permanent disability which disinclined me to the intoxication of tobacco, I could offer but trifling testimony as to the advantage gained by quitting the habit. But it so happened that my general health was good, except as nicotine injured it, which it did constantly and seriously. Therefore, when I experienced a remarkable change for the better morally, mentally and physically, within three months after stopping tobacco, the primary cause of the welcome improvement was easily located, and now that two years have elapsed since I left off the habit the good results of my abstinence are not only more pronounced but have become permanently fixed. I deem it worthy of mention that my cure was wrought by grace of God and will power, and without the slightest aid from nervine medicines or tobacco substitutes.

## This Little Book Is Written:

To prove—That tobacco makes drunkards, because liquor and tobacco are complemental intoxicants, nicotine checking circulation of blood while alcohol temporarily increases it.

To prove—That the young man who smokes loses thereby one-half his chances for success in life, to say nothing of the resultant moral, mental and physical deterioration.

To prove—That middle-aged men who have used tobacco, and are now feeling its unpleasant cumulative effects, can quit the habit, and by so doing be rewarded with revived ambition, enhanced bodily vigor and increased power of intellectual toil. These blessings, if wisely applied, will surely bring many additional years of usefulness and happiness.

To prove—That the Christian women of America who recognize the horror of intemperance can save young men from alcoholic perdition by persuading them to abstain from tobacco, because the young man who smokes has about an even chance of taking to drink, whereas the young man who resolutely rejects tobacco is practically in no danger of becoming a victim of the rum dragon.

The population of the United States increased less than fifty per cent in the last twenty years, while the consumption of intoxicating beverages grew over three hundred and fifty per cent in the same stretch of time. This ominous fact indicates national decadence, while proving that the liquor defense is stronger than the Hence

Yet I have faith that somewhat of my seed-corn will, at the long last, sprout and return increase, even from this reluctant soil, but I fear me that many an autumn shall come and go ere the harvest be garnered in. This hope of an ultimate result is founded on the recollection of what happened in my own case, once upon a time and long ago.

About a quarter of a century since I had reported a social affair in Jersey City for a New York morning paper, and was returning by the Courtland street ferry. I was seated in the men's cabin smoking with much unction, in consequence of an enforced abstinence of several hours' duration, when all at once a gentleman next me broke in on my musings by saying, in low and very kindly tones, "Are you aware that you can slowly but surely smoke away your courage, your ambition, and your power of sustained application? Do you know that nicotine poison is not only the direct cause of many distressing physical ailments, but is frequently the unsuspected agency of defeat in the strenuous competitions of our modern life by lulling men into a contented inertia while the golden chances of honor and success slip through their nerveless fingers?"

It was an elderly man of striking presence who spake and I listened courteously to his warning, which, though I heeded not in act, was for the moment singularly impressive. We chatted a trifle longer, the boat swung into the slip and I parted forever from my unknown mentor.

I was then entirely incredulous that his admonition held the slightest item of prophecy for me, but when at last my young manhood was hull down below the horizon, and the cumulative effects of tobacco robbed my days of usefulness and my nights of ease, I bitterly realized the truth of the old man's counsel.

This illumination came sadly late, but still I gained from it inspiration and purpose that helped me much in the struggle which made me free. Therefore, I do not despair of these words and trust their lesson may find lodgment in the memories of those who shall draw valorous persistence therefrom when their hour of striving after emancipation finally comes.

Of the two classes I hold in particular solicitude I naturally have a nearer personal interest in the middle-aged men, who know the evil of the tobacco habit and would gladly rid themselves of it if they could do so without going through a very uncertain and extremely unpleasant experience. Non-users of tobacco cannot sympathize with them as one can who has been every foot of the hard road whereon these victims of nicotine are now traveling. But in the case of a youth who has not yet formed the habit, all persons of moral sensibility should be of one mind, no matter whether they ever used tobacco or not. I believe the time is near at hand when women and men of educated consciences will feel it as much their duty to labor with a youth who is taking to tobacco as they now do with one who is taking to drink.

The only excuse for good mothers and sisters, who look placidly on while the boys of the family learn to smoke, is their ignorance of the harm that will surely come of it. I say nothing of fathers in this connection, because so many of them, by reason of their own indulgence, cannot make a consistent argument against their boys following the paternal example.

When the women have full knowledge that no young man who uses tobacco can be as healthy, as intelligent, as high in moral aim, or as successful in worldly affairs as he would be if he let it alone, it does seem as if they ought to declare unrelenting war against the blighting weed.

We cultured folk living on the edge of the twentieth century are quite amazed at our ancestors of two or three generations ago for their obtuseness regarding the evil of drink. In those days men through the influence of liquor beat their wives, robbed, murdered, and went to the dogs, just as they do now, but rum was not held responsible. At that time a man did not forfeit the reputation of fine gentleman if he drank himself under the table every night in the week, for it was only puling milk-sops who always kept sober. I doubt if we are any brighter-minded than were those distant kinfolks of ours. The difference is we have looked at dram drinking in

If the drunkard makers are to be routed in the course of the next half century, to the salvation of our country, we must offer battle along new strategic lines.

Keep youths from tobacco and you keep them from drink nine hundred and ninety-nine times out of one thousand. Persuade a drinker to quit tobacco and he will give up liquor of his own accord in a large majority of cases.

It is painful and embarrassing to both parties when a woman tells a man he is in danger of coming to grief through drink, for the greater the truth the worse he hates to be told it, and reform rarely follows the telling, whereas the average man, whether a drinker or not, will listen in perfect good humor to the most urgent plea for him to leave off tobacco and not have his pride hurt, no matter how often the woman he respects renews the argument.

This is a mission that all the good women in America can enter upon at once if they will. A ranchman's wife in the most remote Montana valley could thus help build up a glorified republic.

This work cannot be relegated to associations and conventions, if the awful growth of the rum curse is to be stopped. Millions of devoted women must make it part of their daily duty to labor earnestly with one or more tobacco users. At last their loyal service to God and man must prevail, thereby flanking the liquor brigades, driving them from the land we love the best, and thus rescuing our Christian civilization from deadly peril.

Boston, 1898.
Lester C. Hubbard.


# CHAPTER I.

## Tobacco And Its Bondage.


This work is a fragmentary narration of personal experiences in a tobacco thraldom that lasted more than thirty years, together with a digest of the thoughts and conclusions which came to me during that period and since my emancipation.

I trust it may furnish some additional evidence to temperance people who affirm the close inter-relation between rum and tobacco, while awakening inquiry on the part of sincere reformers who have not as yet clearly seen their intimate connection.

I also desire to say something that shall aid in keeping young fellows from getting into the tobacco habit while helping old ones to get out. I make no appeal to middle-aged men who have not contracted the habit, for the reason that this addiction is rarely formed after a man has passed twenty-five. In the case of those under thirty who are already solidly grounded in the indulgence, I confess my hopelessness of securing any immediate results.

I was a tobacco user during the decade between my twentieth and thirtieth years—as well as for long thereafter —and clearly remember my own invulnerability to all argument; and as it was with me then so will it be with others now. The young manhood season is a high and heady time, wherein the consciousness of present life is so vivid that the mind refuses to sense the inevitable changes of the future. Exuberant youth who finds tobacco an alluring pleasure, with never a bodily pain nor moral reproach to discount its charms, smiles at grim predictions of apoplexy, paralysis or shattered nerves, because these ghastly horrors belong to the old and not to him, for how can he ever become old with the boyhood sunshine on his face and its music in his heart?

reverse, and hence see in it the genesis of many a calamity. One hundred years ago if a talented man died of delirium tremens the horror of it was not charged up against whiskey any more than if lightning had struck him.

A boy today goes insane from cigarette smoking, but tobacco is not thereby indicted as a general evil, but it will be, and in less than a hundred years to come.

Ordinarily the teller of a story of personal incident becomes more or less the hero of his tale. If, when I parted from my sage adviser of the North River ferryboat, I had then and there set my teeth in firm determination never to touch tobacco again, and had held true to the vow from that day to this, I might justly take pride both in my pluck and wisdom. But when it is known that instead of dropping the habit I clung to it from the morning time of young manhood until the afternoon of middle age, my figure does not rise heroic on the scene.

I have, however, one consolation in the premises, I know vastly more about the harm of tobacco than I did a quarter of a century ago and hence can give more effective warning as to its fell entrancement.

CHAPTER II.

Seeking Enslavement.

I began the regular use of tobacco the summer I was twenty, in the year 1863, while soldiering down in the Louisiana lowlands. I say regular use, because in my case, as in most others, a disastrous experiment preceded the permanent formation of the habit.

Healthy boys do not crave tobacco, it is strictly an acquired taste, whose after pleasure must be paid for beforehand with spot cash pain.

When we know that the system of the average youth spontaneously revolts upon first introduction to nicotine, it - seems absolutely impossible that the majority of men in each generation would, of their own volition, deliberately become bond slaves of tobacco. Yet they do, and no familiarity with the fact can banish its uncanny marvelousness, because it is an inversion of the logical order of motives that influence human action.

In the absence of social or moral restraint an easy lapse into alcoholic indulgence is readily understood, for the reason that intoxicating drinks are frequently so cunningly compounded as to immediately fascinate the unaccustomed palate, thereby introducing the subsequent exhilaration in a delightful manner. But where is tobacco's seductive enticement to the physical senses of the neophyte? It has none, and is uniformly revolting to beginners. And yet the majority of youths fall under its spell as soon as they come into the basso-profundo stage of voice, and some even before.

If only the hardened brood of outlaw youngsters took to it, as they do to other evil courses, the wonder would not be so great, but this noxious habit gathers them all in with the impartiality of the old sexton, swooping good, bad and indifferent into a regular dog-pound democracy, where mamma's dainty darlings and the ragged street rangers are jostled indiscriminately together.

In all decent society a youth who tipples is looked at askance. If boys taking to smoke lost caste to the same extent not one well-brought-up lad in a hundred would ever form the habit, because the agreeable taste and pleasant stimulation which are the primary incentives to drink are reversed in the case of tobacco.

It must needs be a powerful attraction which tempts a boy to try tobacco again and again, notwithstanding its nauseousness, until finally the outraged system ceases to revolt against its poison and the despotic habit binds another victim hard and fast.

It seems to me the fundamental cause of this perversion of the normal lies in the circumstance that all along the years of youth enticements to smoke go seductively on before beckoning the way to short cuts that lead quickly to the liberty, consideration and full enfranchisement of young manhood. The jaunty older fellows a boy most admires all smoke, to say nothing of the majority of grown men that the world looks up to.

Thus while a lad cannot hurry on physical growth it is easily within his power to initiate himself into the freemasonry of smokers, and while not a man in stature can proudly feel that he has come into a very essential attribute of one. This spurious manliness especially invites him, because, forsooth, no boy who smokes can be scoffed at as a nambypamby feminine fellow by schoolmates, and who does not remember the stinging potency of ridicule during early years? Furthermore, a vivid curiosity urges him on to taste an enjoyment which older companions pronounce wonderfully delicious after the sickening first attempts are over. And finally, there is the insidious pluck test which challenges the lad to prove his nerve by persisting until he conquers the natural repugnance to tobacco. This trial is after the fashion of a savage tribe, which makes the stripling who aspires after manhood's privileges first show his courage by wearing a mitten filled with ants that are noted as hard biters.

As before remarked, I did not begin the steady use of tobacco until I became a solder in the war, and ascribe my long resistance to a painful, but picturesque experience when I was about fourteen.

My boyhood home, forty years ago, was in a village on the banks of the Mississippi river. In those primitive days builders burned their own lime, and I keenly recollect how the awful collapse sequent to my first cigar sent me reeling into an old lime kiln to get out of view and lie down. It was after dark when I arrived home and upon coming into the lighted dining room I was unanimously voted a sight to behold. But my state was more gracious than that of another boy whose mother found him stretched out on the grass, pallid, moaning and incapable of speech. In an agony of terror she sent for the family doctor and that shrewd gentleman, after fumbling and sniffing at the youth a bit, dryly said, "Been smoking, ain't ye?" The patient feebly nodded, upon which his mamma had a sudden change of emotions, that the youngster smarted for afterward.

This first attempt of mine remained so vivid a memory that it protected me from the tobacco temptations ever present in army life until I had been in the service over a year and had marched a couple of thousand miles campaigning in six southern states. If this active movement had kept up I might not have yielded, even then, but after the capture of Vicksburg I was made a commissioned officer and the regiment went into camp for three months at Transylvania Landing, Louisiana. The torrid heat, the monotonous routine of garrison duty, association with officers all older than myself, all of whom used tobacco, together with a sense of false shame at being an oddity among them, furnished a combination of influences that impelled me to private experimenting.

Nausea gradually ceased, pleasant stimulation took its place, and I stepped forth among my comrades elate over a victory which made me their rough and ready equal and no longer a delicate weakling to be jibed at because tobacco made me sick.

Please bear in mind that my satisfaction over the conquest was full, complete, and without alloy of doubt. The idea that my triumph might ultimate in disaster never suggested itself, and why should it, forsooth? My father was a physician and noted in our county for his scientific attainments. He used tobacco, and all the comment on the habit I ever heard from him, was that it hurt growing boys, leaving it inferential that its use was all right for adults. His authoritative dictum settled tobacco's status on the physical plane.

On pleasant evenings I could look across the way from our house and see the good Presbyterian minister tranquilly puffing his pipe, as he wandered bare headed among the shrubbery, and this clerical endorsement proved there was no moral wrong in the habit. A hundred years ago doctors and preachers would have vouched for rum just as conscientiously, and yet its use was as surely pernicious then as I believe the use of tobacco is today.

After taking the degrees which made me an accepted brother of the tobacco fraternity, my content was supreme. I had climbed the mountain wall and descended into the garden of the gods, where it is always afternoon and the fruits are ever ripe. Henceforth there could be no more tedious hours, for under the beguilement of tobacco they would lose their laggard heaviness, and be filled with lightsome song.

If you fancy I am overstating the beatific hallucination of the young smoker, ask a candid friend who has used tobacco for about five years, and now smokes a half dozen cigars a day to figure up the extent of frontage tobacco occupies in the recreation part of his life. If he be a truthful man he is certain to tell you that the space filled by smoking is more necessary to his comfort and pleasure than all other amusements and relaxations put together.

A novelist told me that if he stopped smoking he would have nothing to look forward to when at church or attending social functions. Congressman Scott, the Erie, Pennsylvania, millionaire, who died suddenly a few years ago, once said he had most delightful anticipations of all his meals for the reason that he knew how good a cigar would taste afterward.

The devotees of the weed find it a universal panacea; if tired they smoke, if rested they smoke, hungry or satiated, sad or merry, solitary or in company, tobacco unobtrusively adjusts itself to all moods and conditions and absorbs the odd minutes as a sponge does water.


CHAPTER III.
In The Toils.


Truly my new kingdom was wide and rich, and furthermore my vanity was gratified because I had met the challenge of nicotine and conquered. I little thought then that I had given myself a despotic master, who was to rob my life of its fairest and most productive years, thereby denying me the career of usefulness and honorable distinction which otherwise would surely have been mine.

In what I have said, or may say, concerning the effects of tobacco on myself, I by no means regard mine as an average typical case; on the contrary, it is exceptional, for probably not more than one tobacco user in fifty consumes it to the same extent that I did.

With intoxicants the range of indulgence is from the man dying of delirium tremens to the one who sips a glass of wine now and then at a banquet, while with the tobacco addiction it grades up from the cigarette fiend, who smokes continuously until he goes insane, to the conservative gentleman who confines himself to one mild cigar after dinner. But smoke much or smoke little, there ever yet was a man who smoked habitually that realized on all there was in him, physically, morally or intellectually, to the same extent that he would if he had let tobacco alone. This affirmation is impregnable. Tobacco is always a bane, and no man ever used it, even to a limited degree, and enjoyed the same high-health that he would without it. Non-smokers and those new in the habit may suggest that I am throwing too much lurid glare on my picture, but men of brains who have used tobacco a score of years will rarely say so.

The inexperienced see whole brigades of good citizens, kind fathers and successful business men smoking regularly and yet not showing its harm by any external sign, whereas not one drinker in a thousand, try he never so cunningly, can keep his degrading indulgence from betraying him.

The tobacco habit is one not necessarily obvious to others; coarse boors can make it offensively so, but with well-bred men it remains a very proper-looking Mephistophelian sort of a vice, with no objectionable visible manifestations, although at the same time it may be manufacturing a plentiful grist of internal ills for the future plaguing of its sedate and well-groomed devotee. It should also be remembered that the cult of middle-aged smokers are not garrulously communicative as to the unpleasant results of their addiction. Even where observant helpmeets find out that nicotine is at last bringing their respective spouses to book, the wives do more guessing than husbands do telling.

Tobacco is an easy-going creditor, and for years the sly usurer never puts in an appearance, but lets the compound interest go on piling up, until finally, on some serene evening, he suddenly confronts his long-time debtor and either demands a payment on account or the lump sum due. If the former, he leaves his stamped receipt in the shape of chronic dyspepsia, or irregular action of the heart, or insomnia, or nervous prostration, or a slight paralytic stroke. But if he wants his debt in bulk on the spot he forecloses with a death stroke of apoplexy or heart failure.

Oh! the tobacco shylock, though gentle and smiling at first, is an unrelenting claimant who always gets his own with increase, and neither bankruptcy court nor Portia's shrewd wit can juggle him out of what is nominated in the bond.

At the time I took up with tobacco I had been fifteen months in the army without drinking intoxicants. My abstinence was not due to moral scruples, although my father was an abstainer and mine was a temperance home. The drink question cut no figure in my case because I had no tendency that way through heredity and no one thought I was in any danger of falling into it. The attitude I held toward rum is well illustrated by the following incident:

In December, 1862, our brigade made a forced march along the line of the Memphis and Charleston Railroad to relieve a fort threatened by a body of Confederate cavalry and artillery. It was two o'clock in the morning before we reached it, dispersed the enemy and began our bivouac in an open field. Just at that time a winter rain set heavily in that made lying down out of the question, so everybody took the storm standing as best they could.

At daylight the colonel ordered the quarter-master to issue a bucket of whiskey to each company. I declined the noggin because my senses revolted at the very smell of the raw commissary whiskey. If it had been diluted and sweetened I might have taken my allowance, but as it was I counted among the few who declined the dram, and thus in a sober state was treated to the astounding spectacle of a gloomy, silent and rain-bedraggled regiment of soldiers almost instantaneously transformed into a laughing, shouting, singing mob. Only one drink apiece was given out, hence the tumult soon subsided-without prejudice to discipline. It is very significant that when I came fully under the tobacco habit my spontaneous repugnance to whiskey vanished, and thereafter the horrible stuff ceased to be offensive and I soon began to drink it with the rest.

I charge tobacco with being directly responsible for the struggle with liquor which lasted a quarter of a century and filled my life with unspeakable desolation, and yet through all the contest I was strangely slow in suspecting its malign agency in my undoing. The intoxications from liquor and tobacco, while differing in degree, are closely akin, and supplement each other. Two hundred years ago, in Virginia, when the owners of tide-water plantations were growing rich by shipping their tobacco crop to England, it was truthfully called the "sot weed."

In a particular manner does liquor temporarily brace up a man suffering the drooping goneness induced by nicotine, and many there be who seek its black magic. My illusion that there was no intimate relation between the habits was because my father used tobacco but never drank, so why should it have that effect on me? But it did, and still does on many another temperament like mine.

It can truthfully be said that while all tobacco users are not drinkers, all drinkers are tobacco users.

I know from my own bitter experience how unceasingly nicotine supplies the incentive to drink. During the many years in which I was striving by will power to get away from the horror of liquor, though I conquered temptation in an hundred desperate battles I was sure to be defeated in the one hundred and first, and that result inexorably followed until I dropped the compromising course, of which I shall hereafter speak, and turned my back forever on the tobacco habit, after which it was no fight at all to dispose of the faint and infrequent inclinations to drink.

I am within the facts when I assert that a youth brought up in an average Christian family, if he does not smoke, is so safe from becoming an inebriate that there is not one chance in a thousand that he will ever use intoxicants as a beverage. On the other hand if the same youth takes tobacco the chances are even that he will take to drink, in which event they are again even that he becomes a drunkard and wrecks his life.

## CHAPTER IV.

### Fate Of A Slave.

I do not say I never would have drank while in the army if I had not first used tobacco, because I am convinced that the enticements which constantly environed me were of such a persistent and alluring character that I must ultimately have yielded, but I am now positively certain that my fall would only have been temporary and when I returned home from the war I would have dropped the use of intoxicants entirely.

How nicotine can generate a craving for drink, that finally hardens into unconquerable habit, is pathetically shown by an incident that came under my own observation.

A veteran of the war, seated in a saloon, drew up a mock petition, wherein he asked the government to grant him a pension of one hundred dollars a month for total moral disability contracted while in the army, which made him of no use to himself or anybody else. When this man enlisted at his New England village home no youth in all the township was held in better repute or had fairer prospects.

To natural endowments above the average he added brilliant scholarship, sound moral principles and irreproachable personal habits. The Sabbath before he marched away to the front he taught the Sunday School Class, of which he was the beloved teacher, for the last time.

The young soldier was brave, ready and buoyant. He was also gifted with the inborn military turn, and the changes which come thick and fast along the rough edges of battle brought him prompt promotion.

He served with distinction on the staff of several general officers, and when the war closed was mustered out with honor. His native town, proud of its young hero, gave him enthusiastic welcome home, and everything of fame and fortune which men most covet could easily have been his by the exercise of ordinary diligence and sobriety. Upon his return those who held him dearest were pained to see that he used tobacco to excess, something he had never touched before the war, and it also soon became sadly evident that the rum habit was heavy on him. He strove to mend his ways, and succeeded for short seasons, only to fall back again deeper than before. He was proud, none the less, and so drifted away to the West, where, among strangers his course held steadily downward, until after many vicissitudes he became a homeless, hopeless bar-room hanger-on.

The grim pleasantry of his pension application showed that beneath a stoical exterior his heart agonized over a wasted life, and it was some comfort in his despair that he could charge his blighted career more to the demoralizing influence of army life than to evil tendencies in his own nature. A few years ago his strong constitution broke down. A comrade took him to a hospital, telegraphed relatives to whom he had been lost for years, so when the end came his body was borne tenderly back to his boyhood home among the Berkshire Hills. There, with life's sorrow and tragedy over forever, he sleeps in the old church yard by the side of his father and mother.

The losses of the Great War will never be fully chronicled on this earth—for the record cannot be complete until it includes the pitiful story of all the soldiers who lost everything that gives true glory to manhood, and returned home ghastly phantasms of the noble youths who marched away. I am thoroughly convinced that the officer whose untimely taking off I have related was held in the course of rum drinking, which finally killed him, by his enormous and incessant use of tobacco.

In my own case, after coming completely under the dominion of the habit I found the mild but sustained exhilaration so pleasant that I also used tobacco constantly. I have now come to the core of my subject, and before summing up the results of tobacco on my physical, mental, and moral being, I wish to anticipate a criticism which will inevitably suggest itself to moderate users of tobacco, who have not as yet detected any harm therefrom. These men will quite naturally say, "Such unreasonable use of tobacco ought to bring a man to grief, but it is absurd to make the consequences in his case or that of the unfortunate officer an argument against smoking judiciously at proper seasons." This is the same style of reasoning used by good deacons of sixty years ago regarding rum, but we will let it pass.

I claim the only way it can be demonstrated that tobacco is hurtful in all man's multiform relations to life is to take an extreme instance wherein its evil is so portentously manifest that it cannot be denied. If it be shown that the inordinate use of tobacco was the motor which pulled one man down to bankruptcy in character, health or business, then our case against the "sot weed" is made out, and it must be accepted that the habit will work injury one way or another in exact ratio with amount of tobacco consumed.

If all men who use tobacco to an injurious extent staggered as they walk along the streets, the more crowded highways would be blocked by them; but they don't, and even in the case of victims whose rum drunkenness is indirectly caused by it, their intoxication is charged to the visible agency of alcohol and not to the hidden one of nicotine.

When it comes to the majority of tobacco users who never indulge in drink to a noticeable extent, it is impossible for the closest observer to estimate the full damage being done by the habit. A man may be an inveterate user of tobacco, and so long as he don't drink, can go on for years, and neither he nor his friends will realize that the addiction has robbed him of from ten to fifty per cent of the all-around success in life which would have been his if he had let tobacco alone.

So precious is the indulgence that men reluctantly acknowledge to themselves that the habit is hurting them, hence all the pride of the man rises up in wrathful protest at the surmise that if he had not wasted time and vitality on tobacco he would be a bigger personage in the world than he is. Yet none the less is this averment true of every tobacco user of forty and upwards who has been addicted to the habit since early manhood. This argument of right should be effective with aspiring youths of twenty who cannot be terrorized into tobacco abstinence by threats of possible apoplexy at sixty.

High-spirited young men who smoke may as well bid "good-bye" to alluring visions of honor and renown, because as a rule the fame and fortune they hunger after will be the rewards of their rivals who are not handicapped by the tobacco habit. Thirty years ago my prospects were fair as the best, but while supine and

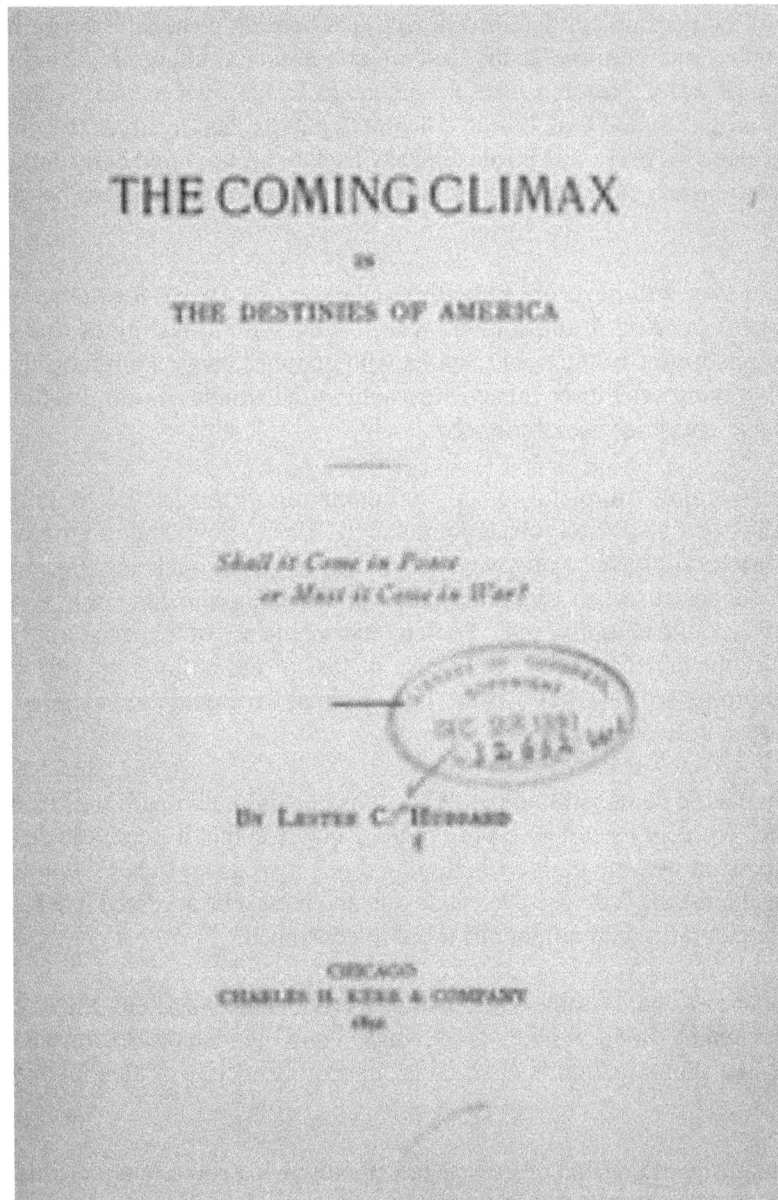

*Lester Hubbard's next, and final, book was about the coming dawn of Revelation and its socio-political impact on the United States. Hubbard couldn't find a publisher in his native Boston to print the book, so he contacted his Chicago-based first cousin **Gardiner Greene Hubbard**, publisher of* National Geographic, *who reportedly printed the book for free and sent them back to Lester C. Hubbard for self-distribution. This makes it a rare book today, as only about 100 copies are known to exist. Apparently, the turn of the century readers Hubbard wrote for were interested in Tobacco, but not theological essays.*

*Gardiner Greene Hubbard died literally within a few days of the book's publication and Lester C. Hubbard died shortly thereafter. He never got to realize his dreams of either a tobacco-free world or the coming of Armageddon.*

lethargic under the benumbing influence of nicotine rich fruits, convenient to my hand, ripened and withered to nothingness, all unpicked.


# CHAPTER V.
## On The Down Grade.


At this distance of time the incidents of my use of tobacco while in the army are sharply defined and in the right perspective. I can now mark out the very month in the fall of 1864 when the lofty ideals I had cherished began to shrink and fade. Am I sure tobacco was the cause of the downward trend of my desires? Absolutely and beyond all question, I am.

From early boyhood I had been a great reader, my temperament was poetic, and the world of material things was scarcely more real to me than the intangible one in which my imagination wandered. Up to the very moment of forming the tobacco habit I had been romantic and ambitious beyond the average and my fifteen months soldiering had accentuated those qualities instead of blurring them. But a single year of tobacco made mournful changes. The horizon, once as wide as the universe, wherein my thought ranged free, was narrowed to the sordid round of a material life destitute of winged aspirations.

Spiritual sentiment became nothing and the animal senses everything. Surely this Circean transformation could only be wrought by a malign power of tremendous potency, but nicotine had evil genii sufficient for the task. Tobacco narcotized my moral nature into a trance as deep as death. The present became all in all, and the future nothing. Pleasures of the mind were ignored and those of the body coddled and petted, and yet I missed not the riches that had gone from me because I knew not my loss, so absorbing was the enchantment of nicotine.

I say again, that this extreme manifestation was due to the fact that I took tobacco in enormous quantities. I freely concede that the man who only consumed a quarter as much would only receive twenty-five per cent of the damage that I did, and it might not be visible either to himself or others, but the ill effects would be entrenched in his system just the same, working a destruction that must surely be revealed in after years.

The pestiferous malaria of the West African Coast often strikes down its victim in a day, while the milder type of a New England marsh may not develop for months, and then only in a slight fever, but both malaria and nicotine at last relentlessly account for themselves in proportion to quantity taken into the organism. The gradual fading away of moral purpose was imperceptible to me, for the reason that men going down hill in character are rarely aware of the circumstance until they stop and try to climb back. Furthermore, the suggestion that he is going to the bad is very offensive to a young man's self love; he resents it from others and is extremely unlikely to discover the fact himself.

Before my first year's novitiate as a tobacco devotee was over I could take my allowance of intoxicants with the thirstiest of them and show no sign. It is your rosycheeked youth with healthy stomach and sound nerves who can put the old fellow to bed. I remember a naval officer of forty-five or fifty that I was out with one night in New Orleans who became maudlin and helpless on an amount of drink that only made me feel blithe, but did that prove I was to escape scot free? Oh, no. I paid the obligation with usury in the after time, just as every young man who now fancies tobacco is not hurting him will find twenty or thirty years hence that he has been running up a score which must be settled to the last nickel.

I liked my duties in the service and had become automatically adjusted to them before I took up with either tobacco or rum, so while in the army nothing occurred to pointedly indicate that a total revolution in character was fast taking place. But in the radical change of environment which followed my muster out at the close of the war a startling decadence is sharply revealed, when I contrast myself at the commencement of my army experience with what I was at the end. In the first place I had not one spark of ambition left, whereas before my enlistment I was aflame with it.

In early youth I warmly fell in with my father's wish that I should become a lawyer. So, after my return home I easily acquiesced in the scheme of beginning my legal studies in Chicago. Not that I intended to buckle down to the dead-wood of the desk and put in time at anything so drearily tedious as studying law—quite the reverse. But going away from home was an escape from parental oversight and made me master of myself, which I truly found a heritage of woe.

At this epoch I had no plans aside from getting all the fun I could out of life each day. I was saturated in tobacco intoxication from morning until night, which circumstance fully accounts for my abnormal outlook on the world. I recall my sincere amazement at young men who were toiling patiently for long hours to build up a business or profession. To my notion they were foolishly throwing away opportunities of immediate pleasure for distant rewards that were dubious, uncertain and of no particular value even when secured.

In my estimation a sober, industrious life was infinitely dismal and without a joy, for if tobacco and intoxicants were eliminated from existence it would not be worth the having. At this period I had a queer fancy which brought me much content. I figured by the doctrine of chances that in all the multiform perils I had encountered while in the army I ordinarily would have been killed, and as I was not it followed quite logically that the remaining years were so much clear gain, and I was therefore fully warranted in giving them exclusively to sport and personal entertainment.

The idea never presented itself that as I had been so strangely spared it was my solemn duty to use the extra time to noble ends. The sodden host which annually slouches down hill to ruin through low self-indulgence, probably does so approvingly, on some sort of a distorted philosophy of life, and I am convinced that in many instances minds drugged by tobacco furnish specious justification for throwing bodies and souls away. For every professional tramp you can produce who does not use tobacco I will undertake to find a white blackbird.

A formidable and malignant influence must have been at work when an idealistic youth enters the army, rises to be an officer, comes home with honor and then deliberately seeks a low level of porcine enjoyment, and remains there contentedly until imperious pains and penalties drive him up and out.

If I had returned from the war addicted to drink alone, and without the tobacco habit, I am certain that the headaches, shame and loss of caste following a few indulgences would have turned me to the rectitude and decencies of life in short order. We know what an important part minor items play in determining our daily round of thoughts and emotions. The black morning depresses and the bright one elevates our spirits. An indigestion or neuralgia brings gloomy forebodings, while a tingling sense of health makes the future rosy with hope. If trifles like these temporarily twist and warp the feelings and anticipations, may we not expect permanent deviations from normal reasoning in the case of a man constantly charged with nicotine?

The first shock of a large portion of alcohol, or even opium, is scarcely greater to the unaccustomed user than that of tobacco. They are alike poisons, and yet through habit the patient and long-suffering organism tolerates them all in varying degrees of forbearance. The illusions of the drunkard or opium-eater are rightly placed in the borderland of insanity. While the major effects of tobacco are diffused and held in abeyance for future cumulative action, the lesser ones are frequently enough to make a man's plan of life irrational, as in my case. I delighted in the tobacco stimulus, and, expecting no injury therefrom, used it so incessantly as to be steeped in its semi-intoxication, whether sleeping or waking.

Rum, opium or tobacco when taken continuously and immoderately, show they are closely akin, the only difference being in the degree of immediate effect. In the case of excessive users of rum or opium there is total lack of working capacity, and death or insanity makes the tragedy a short one. With the extreme use of tobacco these finalities are much longer coming, while their approach is less obvious, but they unerringly arrive at last.

An Oriental traveler states that a majority of high-grade Chinese business men smoke opium every night, but rigidly abstain during the day. It is said these cautious Confucians despise the opium fiend who smokes at all hours, as much as our gentlemen, who confine themselves to a bottle of wine at dinner, do a vagabond perennially drenched in whiskey.

Rum, opium, and tobacco are supreme intoxicants of the world they devastate. Use to excess and you are on the railroad to swift ruin. Use moderately, and while the harm done may remain hidden for years, the poison must ultimately register its evil force somewhere within your life. In consequence of my unthinking abandonment to tobacco, I illustrated what its full effect can be in the case of an impressible, emotional, young man of unformed character, with whom early religious training had become merely a vague reminiscence.

Nicotine acted on me as a mental opiate, and I laughed at the suggestion of working and denying myself in the present for rewards of money and fame in the future. It was also a moral opiate which closed my ears to the imploring plea of conscience, so that, when drugged by it, I became the spoil of other vices which prey on young manhood.

Thus was I, just before my twenty-third birthday, with neither hope nor fear for the future, seeking jubilantly the way of sin and death, without one sigh of remorse, without one lingering regret after the noble life that might have been, and without one thought of the inexorable day of doom which was to dawn for me in this world, when I should find my accuser, my judge and the condemned in one and the same person.


CHAPTER VI.
The Nicotian Beguiler.


If the subtle genius of tobacco should become incarnate and appear before an assembly of youths who were wavering as to whether or no they better take to smoking, he might make persuasive speech as follows:

"The use of my wonder-working weed belongs to the modern world of progress and invention. Two hundred and fifty years ago probably not over two hundred and fifty thousand people regularly availed themselves of its transcendent virtues. Now not less the than two hundred and fifty million of its devotees would be conscious of an aching void of vast dimensions if tobacco were instantly annihilated off the face of the earth. This circumstance shows that it fills a long-felt want, the same as beer and whiskey. If ye become my liegemen you will never be lonesome nor lack for company. While if nervous, troubled or ill at ease you will spontaneously turn to my precious specific for sure relief. Now, for this miracle-working gift I only ask a percentage out of your lives and agree to subtract it in such a smooth manner that not one in a thousand of you will ever miss it or even be aware that I have conveyed it away."

This deft magician would probably make no mention as to the nature of the percentage which he so artfully filches, but we can positively inform all curious young gentlemen that it is taken from innocence of heart, buoyant hopes, noble aspirations, pure morals, personal beauty, health of body, strength of mind, grace of manner, distinction in study, skill and endurance in athletics, and power of regular application. Wherever nerve, courage or readiness of resource are demanded the smoking boy is always behind the nonsmoker of equal endowments and is surpassed by him in scholarship as well as in all competitive tasks requiring unflinching determination.

In several institutions where statistics have been kept non-smoking scholars grade fifty per cent higher in study than those who use tobacco. At West Point and Annapolis it is noted that every year an increasing number of cadet candidates are rejected on account of tobacco heart. In this connection I am considering the average youth, and not the phenomenal marvel, who gains prizes and keeps at the head despite rum and tobacco, but who ultimately goes all to pieces at once. I am aware that arguments and facts proving the disastrous results of tobacco carry little weight with the average boy, or man either, for that matter, but what high spirited youth would wish to take on a habit which, again and again, has paved the way to drunkenness, use of narcotics and finally to crime, imbecility, insanity and early death?

A distinguished German physician declares that one half the male deaths in Germany between the ages of eighteen and thirty-five are due to smoking. A French authority avers it to be the immediate cause of insanity in many cases by developing latent tendencies in that direction. Another physician is of the opinion that tobacco is more harmful than alcohol, because its use is more general, and its effects less obvious. A famous alienist says that paresis, or softening of the brain, is in many instances referable to tobacco only.

It is a matter of scientific record in sanitariums, where the mentally unbalanced are treated, that very often as soon as patients are broken of the tobacco habit, vertigo, insomnia, melancholia, and suicidal impulse vanish, because these complaints were exclusively due to tobacco intoxication. It is a singular fact that while those insane from alcohol when cured acknowledge rum as the cause, tobacco lunatics can rarely be convinced, and so take up the habit again. French medical men affirm that tobacco is helping depopulate France, as the children of inveterate smokers are puny, stunted in stature, and short-lived.

Dr. Bremer, of the St. Vincents Institution for the Insane at St. Louis, denounces tobacco as the deadly enemy of healthy brains. He says all its fascination is in its toxic effect, and knowing the wide-spread ruin wrought by it, believes that if teachers, preachers, and physicians united in pronouncing anathema on tobacco, the laity would heed their warning.

In 1856 a committee from the Queen's College of Physicians at London reported that seven out of nine cases of paralysis and apoplexy came from tobacco, it being far worse than alcohol in causing heart failure, and furthermore, that liver troubles, nervous irritation, dyspepsia, decayed teeth, deafness, and cancer, all came from it.

This brings to mind the case of Gen. Grant, done to death by tobacco cancer at sixty-three, when both his parents lived to be nearly ninety. Robert Louis Stevenson burnt his lungs out with excessive smoking, thus killing himself before he had reached his prime. These tragedies show the progressive nature of the deadly habit, for the man moderate with tobacco today may be using it enormously within a year.

If all the men untimely cut off by nicotine had the fact carved on their tombstones, "Killed by Tobacco" would be a frequent legend in our cemeteries. Some thirty years ago Dr. John H. Griscom, an eminent physician of New York City, gave it as his opinion, as the result of the close observation of a half century, that "Tobacco is steadily producing more diseased bodies, and causing more deaths than all other intoxicants put together." Tobacco checks the circulation of the blood, while alcohol temporarily increases it, which accounts for many tobacco users' strong tendency toward alcoholic beverages. It likewise makes it easy to understand why ninety-five per cent of the members of an English temperance society who returned to drink were smokers.

Where a youth has no fear of physical ill results, he ought to let tobacco alone if, convinced that its use will imperil his prospects in life. I do not believe it possible for even a total abstainer from intoxicating drink to use tobacco in a limited way for twenty years without beating himself out of at least ten per cent of the all-around success which otherwise would have been his.

There is a sly, beguiling quality in tobacco which brings crafty influences to bear on a man's volition, thereby swindling him out of his own. It coaxes him not to overdo, lures away his energy and dulls the ardent interest in his work, by which alone men gain first place in any vocation.

Smoking during business hours is now barred everywhere, hence the smoker is often impatient of his toil, wishing the day done and season of indulgence begun.

The flaming enthusiasm by which the great deeds of earth are mainly wrought, quickly dies out amid the slumbrous fumes of nicotine. Tobacco makes a man satisfied with holding his job or keeping his place in the procession. It bids him be content where he is and discourages forging ahead to grander conquests.

Of all masters tobacco is the most despotic. It possesses the bodies of its slaves when present and their thoughts when absent.

## CHAPTER VII.

### The Tobacco Tyrant's Exactions.

There are in every community large numbers of good husbands and fathers, honored citizens, successful business men and total abstinence church members, who use tobacco and don't seem the worse for it. Very true; but you never observe one of them standing on the street corner advising young men to take up the habit. On the contrary, all declare it hurtful and wish they were well rid of it. These men, as a rule, have strong minds and are firm set in righteous ways, and yet the downward draft of nicotine toward inertia makes them brace sharply in resistance and thus squander force from which no results of worth ever come back.

Tobacco makes tasks harder to do. Hence if a smoker's business affairs are kept in proper shape it exhausts about all his energy and there is no surplus for public duties or altruistic endeavor. Other things being equal, a business man without the habit and one with are in comparative capacity for exacting service, like two persons ascending a mountain, one free of all encumbrance and the other with a twenty-five pound knapsack strapped to his back.

A commercial disaster is more liable to unnerve the tobacco user, who will worry and smoke while the other fellow, free from tobacco, is up and grappling with his fate. Tobacco takes the spontaneous valor out of a man, leaving him in bad form to front vexing emergencies. So long as business moves on with automatic regularity the smoker is apparently as good a man as any, but let a sudden break occur, that demands instant attention, then his weakness declares itself. Many and many a total bankruptcy is due to the smoker's indecision, lack of ready courage and failure in prompt action at the critical moment.

Everyone knows that in these times of intense competition, financial success or failure are frequently determined by the presence or absence of calm judgment, unfailing good humor, ready tact and diplomatic self-control. The chances are greatly against the nicotine victim having these potent agencies constantly in stock. On the contrary, he is liable to be querulous and fretful, trifles upset him, he speaks the hasty word out of season and unduly magnifies the minute disagreeables that inevitably crop up in the daily round, while far oftener than the non-smoker he lacks that equability of temper and serene poise which are such strong cards in the game of life.

A middle-aged man who fails in business, under ordinary circumstances should soon recover his grip and start in again. But how often it is that an unobtrusive gentleman is pityingly pointed out as one who met a commercial reverse and has never been able to get on his feet again. But, oh! how industriously he smokes and smokes and smokes.

These are actual results of the habit and not fanciful theories, and therefore ought to be influential in making non-smoking youths shun the tobacco blight. It is axiomatic that all persons seek happiness according to their best judgment, which frequently, however, is sadly at fault. The youth who takes tobacco for the joy of it passes under the rule of a jealous tyrant, who banishes many pleasures that once were dear to him. He no longer delights in fruits, ices or dainty dishes as he once did, but there is a dubious compensation in this case, for without a shudder he can swallow down the vilest tasting medicines, which before he used tobacco would nearly have thrown him into spasms.

Then, again, the little games and merry romps of the home circle have lost their old-time charm. He thinks it is because he is getting to be a man, while the true reason is that nicotine has so dulled his gentler sensibilities that the simple recreations of other days seem childish or stupid. Observe closely and you will notice that the boy who smokes much soon loses sparkle and vivacity. He becomes somber-mannered, laughs less frequently, and when he does the blithesome ring is nearly all gone out of it.

The number of homes whose happiness is marred by the nervous irritability of smoking husbands is beyond computation. The career of the great Carlyle points a pungent moral to this statement. He was one of the mighty geniuses of the ages. Vast in brain and abounding with nerves, the precise organization to which tobacco is an active poison, and yet he smoked from youth up, darkening all his manhood years with pain and sorrow, while making living with him a dismal tragedy for his wife, once the brilliant and winsome Jane Welsh. His mother smoked before he was born and on all his home visits mention is made of their tobacco symposiums. In Froude's biography of him, extracts from scores of Carlyle's letters are given, and almost every one contains growlings and groanings over his personal woes:

*"Didn't sleep an hour last night, got up and smoked till nearly daylight and still sweet slumber came not. Rest ruined next night by the crowing of a cock a half mile away, while dogs, pianos and milkmen agonize him until he wishes he were dead."*

It took him thirteen years to write the life of Frederick the Great, because months would go by without his putting a line on paper in consequence of nervousness and general incompetency for persistent toil. Carlyle must have suspected the harm that smoking was doing him, for he writes of the habit as follows:

*"Influences generally bad, pacificatory- but bad, engaging you in idle, cloudy dreams, or, still worse, promoting composure among the palpably chaotic or discomposed. Soothing all things into lazy peace, that all things may be left to themselves very much and to the laws of gravity and decomposition."*

The anguish in which he wrought his literary tasks filled Carlyle with horror both before and after their doing. How different with our own Prescott, who, nearly blind during his entire career as a writer, and doing his work despite heartrending drawbacks, nevertheless asked that after death his body should rest a few hours in the library where he had labored through so many happy years.

On my twenty-third birthday, although I had used liquor and tobacco to excess for about two years to my great moral and mental detriment, no painful physical results had as yet declared themselves, but this pleasing condition of affairs was not destined to long continuance. My system at last revolted at the persistent abuse. The morning finally came when I awoke feeling decidedly miserable, and ever thereafter if I drank heavily one day I was certain to be sick the next. I emphatically begrudged so large a payment for fun done and over with and thenceforward strove to keep my indulgence within such judicious limits as would secure all the pleasures of intoxication, while escaping its pains. I was never able to make this shrewd combination, though I tried for years to bring it about.

I soon noticed when recovering from a lapse, by the rigid regimen of temporary total abstinence from drink, that I used more tobacco than customary, although my ordinary allowance was excessive. I also observed several years later that the effects of tobacco delayed my getting well. Then commenced a very peculiar but exceedingly desperate conflict with my drink tendency.

If my faculties had not been constantly drugged by nicotine, I should soon have ceased the use of intoxicants forever, because, after a few experiments in my normal state, it would have become unmistakably evident that alcohol was intensely antagonistic to my nervous make-up. But I failed then to discover the fact, so the years went by filled with battle on battle, defeat on defeat, agony on agony. Very frequently I would go a month without touching a drop of liquor, successfully fighting off tobacco's perpetual incitement to it a score of times for every once that I fell.

Finally it came to me that tobacco was the secret enemy who wrought my undoing, and I formed the resolution to quit both drink and tobacco for ten years, thinking by the expiration of that period my system might be so changed that I could return to a moderate indulgence in both, and avoid the disagreeable after effects which go with their extreme use. By a Titanic exercise of will-power, I quit tobacco and drink short off, took neither substitutes nor medicines, and in a few weeks came into such health as I had not known since boyhood. But my motives had no loftiness of purpose, so my fine-spun scheme after working to a charm for three months suddenly collapsed. It failed by reason of the absence of that moral force through which alone man resists temptation when the inevitable black day comes, that at one time or another intrudes itself into all lives.

*"The world looked dark and dreary/And life was full of pain,*
*My soul grew sick and weary/So I got drunk again."*

I soon pulled myself together, however, quit both toxins again, and started in again with unshaken faith that my patent contraption of a long season of abstinence would ultimately enable me to indulge with discretion on a safe basis. During the ensuing ten years, I probably suffered the anguish, and it is anguish, of leaving off tobacco and drink twenty different times, ceasing their use all the way from two weeks to two months.

At last a supreme might came into my life. I awoke in the lone mid hours, and through the starry silence a still, small voice whispered into the deeps of my soul, " You are sinning against God who made you. You are sinning against your own immortal spirit. You are sinning against your brother man, whom it is your duty to help." From that night, I never touched tobacco nor any other intoxicant.

Before I took my first recess from tobacco its cumulative effects began to show themselves. Up to that time the unpleasant physical results were limited to "that gone feeling" and a slight nervousness. These conditions were usually developed along toward evening, but a night's slumber banished them, and the next morning found me fresh and keen for another day's revel with nicotine. This reaction gradually became more intense and complex, as insomnia, bilious troubles and other painful manifestations put in an appearance. Furthermore, in exact proportion as these discomforts grew, the fascinating stimulation waned, until only a shadow of the old-time pleasure survived; but the imperious habit was still there, and seemingly more powerful than ever.

Just before my permanent victory it was fully as much misery to take tobacco as it was to let it alone, but my now unmasked tyrant made me use it all the same, until I fought myself free from him. By this time I was not taking more than a quarter as much as I did at thirty, but it was enough to furnish me a whole cargo of agonizing symptoms, utterly unknown twenty years before. This cumulative effect unrelentingly follows the long-continued use of tobacco and is the Nicotian Hell that awaits those who keep up the habit beyond middle age.

Immediately before my complete emancipation, I was troubled with irregular action of the heart to an alarming extent, my unrefreshing slumbers were broken by hideous nightmare dreams, while I was morbidly despondent and incapable of regular work.

CHAPTER IX.

Breaking My Bonds.

In my former temporary triumphs over the tobacco habit, I conquered through dogged determination alone. My final and decisive battle was won by a re-enforcement from that power in the Universe which maketh for righteousness.

I asked for help and help came.

By reason of many experiences, I am past master of the pangs and queer sensations which go with breaking loose from the tobacco habit and have likewise pioneered the wilderness that must be traversed before the land of promise can be gained. Hence for the guidance of fugitives who may hereafter start on the desperate journey, I will blaze a trail through the pathless jungle, at the same time locating the snares and pitfalls which beset the way, and also indicate where lions of horrid front may be expected to bound out for the purpose of frightening the wayfarer back into bondage.

Many men who know tobacco is injuring them and therefore try to quit it, soon fall away, because, after stopping a day or two, they find themselves in unknown territory, floundering around in a dense mist, over a rugged stretch of country that has no roads, and all the while feeling so lost and miserable they would give boot to die. Quitting liquor is not nearly so difficult, for then a man knows the nature of the excursion and can mark his progress, but in the case of tobacco the pilgrim is often in a bog up to his ears, with no clearly defined idea as to how or when he can get out.

If he be escaping from drink, his dear ones may extend intelligent aid, while sustaining him by their love and sympathy, but when it comes to tobacco emancipation the patient knows he is in the fight all alone. Those nearest him, try they never so hard, can do but little save speak words of encouragement in a colorless, perfunctory manner. His wife and children are aware that shame, ruin and death do not enter into the struggle, as they would in the case of liquor, so they cannot take as intense an interest in the outcome. Furthermore, the head of the house while going through the ordeal may have paroxysms of nervous fussiness that will make the whole family quite reconciled if he returns to smoking. And all this time the lone wanderer is drearily conscious that not a single human being realizes the stupendous tragedy he is going through.

A man stopping tobacco should arrange for at least a week's vacation from business, for I can positively assure him that his new job will furnish all the work he can conveniently attend to during that time. I advise that no recourse be had either to substitutes for tobacco or nervine medicines, for the reason that a man stands a better chance to stay cured if he goes through without them. There is no sense in taking on a new habit to kill off an old one.

The modern degenerate is a creature of pernicious habits, and the man desirous of being sound in body and mind should above all things get out of the habit of having a habit that is injurious, for one bad habit is almost certain to bring in others.

We will suppose the patient takes his last cigar to-night. It is a common experience with the veteran smoker, though feeling the nicotine victim's heavy dullness on awakening, to be quite brisk after his morning's repast, but the first cigar promptly burns out the vitality stored up over night and the delightful elasticity of feeling vanishes for the day. On the crucial morning, two hours after breakfast and no cigar, the experimenter feels brighter and more buoyant than he has in years, when he smoked immediately after eating. He continues to improve throughout the forenoon, and near mid-day is liable to have an agreeable lightness in the head, as if some mild exhilarative had been taken. About this time he is ready to club himself for not quitting the habit ages ago, the task being so fascinatingly easy. This illusion, however, is decidedly evanescent, and along in the afternoon the yearning for a smoke becomes unpleasantly insistent.

I usually found that five o'clock in the afternoon of the succeeding day marked the hour of my first sharp encounter with the enemy. The tobacco dragon seemed to encircle my body with constrictive coils, which it tightened up now and then, as if in warning that it was there to stay until torn off piecemeal. Getting rid of the immediate effect of excessive alcoholic indulgence is accompanied by a collapse which frequently keeps the victim in bed. In all my experiences with quitting tobacco there never was a hint of weakness. I ate more than usual and waxed steadily stronger physically, but I was possessed by a nervous uneasiness that cannot be described and must be felt to be understood.

Profound dissatisfaction with existence in its every detail rapidly ensued, while, from no cause in particular, I grew madder and madder at things in general. The rhinoceros is said to be the only animal that is constantly in a state of truculent rage. I hereby warn wives that husbands stopping tobacco, for the time being are like unto this ferocious pachyderm and become overflowing vials of wrath which must be handled very gingerly.

My advice to patients, in the first skirmish with the habit, as well as in all subsequent pitched battles which must be fought before freedom is gained, is: be active; seek company; play games; keep your mind employed; go to places of amusement; tire yourself by excercise; eat the instant you have an appetite; and above all, avoid morbid introspection by filling your hours so full you have no time to watch your case.

The second night after quitting is usually one of piebald experiences. There is a slight headache and odd twinges of pain show up in varies portions of the anatomy. Sleep is broken into short naps, wherein come weird and fantastical dreams, but the agony is as nothing to that endured by a man recovering from a drinking bout.

The evening and the morning make the opening of the second day, and with a man of invincible resolution the most desperate part of the contest is over. For some days thereafter the pronounced symptoms are restlessness, snappishness of temper, and a bewildering sense that the customary routine of existence has been turned topsy turvy. Persistent abstinence will conquer this plague of disagreeables in one week, but the sufferer cannot by any means be positively convinced of the fact, therefore during four or five days the situation is critical, the patient being liable to drop all holds at any moment and fall back into the clutches of his old tyrant.

I think the special danger of lapsing at this period is due to the reflex action of a sudden invasion of sensations alike new and odious. An unfamiliar environment worse by far than all the rest. The the old accustomed life has vanished and the seeker after freedom finds himself in a ghastly under-world filled with nightmare material. As the laggard hours go by without bringing relief the great yearning after the well-known realities comes over him. He concludes that the day of possible reformation has passed and hence it would be folly to give the few remaining years of life to fruitless agony. So he surrenders; as to an inexorable fate, lights the magic cigar that puffs . or out the new and puffs in the old, while the tricky tobacco sprites he knows so well merrily prepare their pincers and thumbscrews.

I can assure the wayfarer who so soon lost nerve, that just a little longer endurance would have brought him happily out of the barren desert into the richness of the promised land. If the pilgrim valorously persists at this critical juncture, on the fourth morning his head will be clearer than for many a year, and a sharp-set appetite will furnish delightful intimation that the vigor of other days is coming back again. After the first week, tobacco's continuous temptation will be gone, although it may appear at the usual times of indulgence and also bob up unexpectedly during the day; but these presentations will become less frequent, until they entirely cease. The first wholesome result of abstinence to strongly impress you will be the sweet sleep that comes with the night, and when a month has passed you will no longer miss a smoke after meals, and thus the tobacco curse will fade out of your life.


# CHAPTER X.

Blessed Emancipation.

When I ceased tobacco permanently I was in a generally shattered condition, and had also arrived at an age when the system does not rally from sickness or depression as it did earlier, yet within four weeks insomnia, irregular action of the heart and indigestion no longer troubled me as formerly. I had suffered from debility until I could not walk a mile without great fatigue. An hour's steady writing wore me out, while my mind was baffled by tasks demanding close study and concentration of thought. In less than three months after quitting tobacco I could walk miles with ease, while my mental and bodily powers were equal to any reasonable amount of labor.

I never realized how much time tobacco squandered until I was free from it. Then, all at once, I came into possession of two or three extra hours a day whose very existence was unknown to me so completely had smoking befogged them. The languid reveries induced by nicotine, out of which no good ever came, were replaced by seasons of energized thought that produced valuable returns. The will to do and the soul to dare, so long narcotized to inaction and timidity, awoke to high ambition and bold resolve, while the glad buoyance of other days came back from the past and thrilled me as of old.

Tobacco takes hope and spriteliness out of the young, so what must it do to men on the western slope of life. A tobacco-using poet of great genius, upon arriving at three score, drearily sang:

*"The Spring hath less of brightness
And the snow a ghastlier whiteness*

*Every year.*

*Nor do Summer flowers quicken,
Nor Autumn fruitage thicken
As they once did, for they sicken*

*Every year."*

Tobacco intensifies every physical symptom of old age and deepens the shadow of its oncoming night. The man in middle life, who is not a confirmed invalid, upon quitting tobacco will note with wonder and delight that for him the miracle of miracles is being wrought and time is rolling backward to the sunrise years when heart and the world were young., His step grows brisk, the heaviness of toil departs, and no longer shrinking from hard tasks he easily masters them.

There is charm in a multitude of social doings that had no interest for him when under tobacco, and the society of family and friends develop new attractions as he himself gains in cheeriness and patience. Then, if so be it by reason of growing infirmities he gloomily thought nevermore to enter the arena where worldly success is fought for and won, what a bounding at the heart is his upon realizing that again has come to him the courage high and muscle strong, and that again he can fearlessly plunge into the storm of war where the press of knights is thickest and the crash of battle roars loudest.

I would remind sufferers skeptical of this happy outcome of a fight fought long ago in sunny Italy. It raged far beyond the noon hour, and the French legions crumbled and gave back before the massed Austrian brigades. Said Napoleon to Dessaix: "Well, the battle is lost." "Yes," replied the valiant young general, "this battle is certainly lost, but it is only four o'clock and there is still time to win another one before dark."

And Marengo became the gateway to Bonaparte's dazzling destiny. So you tobacco men with whom it is "four o'clock in the afternoon" eliminate nicotine, and mayhap for you there is another battle and another victory. Persons of a conservative order of mind, who suspect all extreme statements, will probably deem my recital of the good results of quitting tobacco to be overwrought, exaggerated and largely fanciful. To those doubting ones I can only reply that such was the outcome in my own case, and I believe it will prove approximately true with all middle-aged men who are in good health except as nicotine injures them. Of course the physical make-up of the patient exercises a modifying influence, because the bilious, phlegmatic man is not hurt by tobacco as is one of nervous, sanguine temperament, while it is easier for him to stop.

It should be remembered, however, that the swarthy, stolid adipose individual, with cast-iron stomach, skull an inch thick, and no nerves, is not grown on this continent to any large extent at the present time. On the contrary, we are rapidly evolving a distinctively American type that is fine-strung, delicately organized and endowed with a brain having more convolutions than that of the average European. To this new order of man nicotine is especially hostile, but, if it has not broken his system beyond repair, just as soon as the poison is entirely eliminated and the patient comes into normal health, the contrast between what he was when under the fell dominion of tobacco, and what he becomes after a year of freedom and abstinence, is as striking as glorious.

The physical and mental change for the better which stopping tobacco can bring to young men is powerfully illustrated in the case of certain students who came under the benign influence of the great Horace Mann. In the Fall of 1853 this distinguished educator left his seat in Congress, and, refusing the nomination for Governor of Massachusetts, accepted instead the Presidency of Antioch College in the State of Ohio. Mrs. Mary Mann, in the admirable biography of her noble husband, writes as follows:

*"During that year Mr. Mann devoted much time to the cure of many habits in the students common to Western society, among which the indiscriminate use of tobacco was very prominent. Mr. Mann has been thought unduly severe upon this habit, which is not surprising when its evil is so little recognized by the world in general. But perhaps even such critics would have sympathized with him there, for recitation rooms and even parlors were rendered almost uninhabitable by the vile accompaniments of chewing and smoking.*

*For several months he spent every evening he could command in using his moral and persuasive influence to induce the students to renounce the practice, and succeeded so far that before the end of the first college year all but three students signed the pledge to discontinue its use. In some cases the reform was very striking, for young men who had been addicted to the habit from youth up were changed from sallow, nerveless, irritable, stupid individuals, painful to behold, to fair, strong, cheerful seekers after knowledge and happiness!"*

Mrs. Mann's testimony as to the transforming effect of tobacco abstinence is certainly as positive and emphatic as my own. Emerson says: "If you desire fame, wealth, knowledge or virtue, pay the price and take it." You slaves who would be free from tobacco bondage, tell down the coin of endurance and determination and you can buy release. Is it worth the purchase price of denial and misery? Aye, it is, and a thousand times over.

All the brutalizing delights that fifty years of alcoholic indulgence can give would be dearly bought by one night of the drunkard's agony. On the other hand, the man who was in the slow torment stage of the tobacco habit and has fought his way out will tell you that one year of continuous suffering would be a small price to pay for the relief and joy of a full emancipation, because the pain was temporary while the blessing that came after it is permanent.

But beyond and above all these passing and earthly considerations tower those imperishable ones that have to do with the immortal spirit. Life is a march and a battle, wherein the soul must toil unceasingly to gain the grace it covets, because every step toward sublimer heights is made from the conquest of some sin or weakness in the lower man. A good Christian who uses tobacco and knows that it limits his capacity for worthy service may say: "The struggle to stop is more than I can go through; my course of life is nearly run, and I will soon be where the tobacco temptation cannot follow me." Very true; but there will be one flaw in perhaps an otherwise perfect character which must be made good even in Heaven. The lessons God sets cannot be shirked by dying, and sometime and somewhere the tasks are sure to be placed before us again, and, while new in form, will be just as hard to learn as were the old.

CHAPTER XI.
A Call To Action.

The noble women who are unselfishly working at the evolution of a higher humanity have a right to ask aid of all good men, but it will rarely be given by those habitually under the influence of nicotine. No matter how strenuous the efforts of a minority, it cannot carry on its back the dead weight of an inert majority. If the earnest few fail to energize the many into beneficent action with them the forward movement of mankind stops, as it did for centuries during the Dark Ages. All through that long night of sloth there were fruitful souls who nurtured the seed which afterward flowered into the Renaissance, but there were not enough of them to leaven the inert mass of their own day.

It took a majority of the American people to abolish slavery, and temperance never gained a victory in any community where the main body of its citizens were not actively on its side. The amazing development of the last fifty years, while multiplying the precious resources of our civilization, has correspondingly increased the perils which always menace the social order. The owner of a mud hut in the wilderness has little need of worriment over the security of his meager belongings, but let him come into possession of a palace filled with fragile treasures and his watch and ward must be unceasing.

Never, in all the history of our country, were the services of a mighty host of unselfish workers so urgently demanded. And where can they be recruited? Where are the soldiers waiting to be mustered for the new crusade? The women are doing grandly in the organization of clubs and societies for uplifting and redeeming, but women alone cannot grapple successfully with the heavy tasks which confront the coming generation. They must have the help of millions of brave, high-souled, sound-bodied men or they will fail, and if they do fail the night shadows into which so many weak and wicked civilizations of the past vanished may close darkly round our own.

Please count the tobacco-using men of your acquaintance who are active in any kind of benevolent work of a systematic character, requiring time and toil regularly administered, and you will find them very few indeed. Such men upon impulse can devote themselves for a brief time to good work that is soon over, and that is usually their limit, for the smokers' leisure hours as a rule are inexorably mortgaged. Good people interested in charitable enterprises find the evening particularly suitable, because then there is no interference with the business demands of the day. But how is it with our smoking gentleman? Wives are frequently heard to say: "It is almost impossible to get my husband out nights; if he does go with me to a lecture, concert or social entertainment he is uneasy as a fish out of water until we get back home."

In many cases this husband who is such an ardent lover of his own fireside is also a tobacco devotee, who recoups himself for denials during the day by a gorgeous revel at night. It is a hard job to secure any of this man's evenings for philanthropic work, and if he does by a great wrench tear himself away from his cigar he will not be in a mood to give efficient help while grudging every minute lost from his pet enjoyment.

Moreover, the tobacco user is rarely a working reformer. Wrapped in his narcotic haze, he can dream out all sorts of Altrurias and Utopias, but it is useless to expect any sacrifice on his part to make them materialize. It is deplorable that the honorable men of America, who of right should be its "directive intelligences," do more and more neglect this first duty as voting citizens. Only a small percentage of this class attend the primaries, and through their absence the rule of our larger cities passes into the hands of the "boss," with his following of machine politicians. I firmly believe the benumbing inertia of tobacco, which holds so many of the good men of our land in its tentacles, is more responsible for their lapse in civic obligations than all other causes combined.

The enlightened woman knows that rum is hostile to her tenderest and holiest interests, and therefore makes unrelenting war against it. She should also know that tobacco is a foe equally as dangerous and far more subtle. Tobacco rivals woman's influence in the home and likewise obstructs the moral reforms wherein lies the progress of the race. Hence, it is woman's fitting mission to promote enlistments in the army of the new emancipation which shall go forth to give it battle. Youths with chivalric ideals quickly respond to the urgency of those whom they romantically admire, or reverently honor, and with this class woman's success as a recruiting officer can be instant and enduring. By gaining a majority of the young as they grow into honorable manhood, in less than two generations the majority of the best men in all communities will be abstainers from tobacco.

STE

# Right now, Doug Rogers is online pretending to be an 18 year old Russian girl.

Sometimes he's a Filipino orphan girl trying to make her way to the United States. Other times he's a North African girl being held against her will by evil pirates.

See, Doug gets money from rich older men. He scams them into thinking that if they continue to send money to the "girl" in peril, she'll come running into his arms and marry him, and they'll live happily ever after.

Little do the victims know that on the other side of he computer monitor lies the face of a crook. Little do they know that directly to the left of his computer monitor lies a can of Copenhagen Snuff.

Not only is Douglas a scammer, he's also a snuffer. And the money that these men send him helps to maintain his three-can- a-day habit and his frequent trips to the dentist.

Will Doug be caught one day? Who knows. But right now, "Olga Kylashnikov" is getting $10,000 wired to her bank in Ohio. Next week, it will be another $10,000. In the meantime...

## Doug Rogers is a snuff taker.

## The Ephemeris is his magazine.

Reserve your copy of The Snuff Taker's Ephemeris today at www.snuffmagazine.org.

HAPPIER, HEALTHIER, RICHER, THINNER (AND BETTER SEX) THROUGH ALCOHOL

# DRINK THIN

ANTHONY W. HADDAD

"Never in my life DID I think that being an alcoholic could be so HEALTHY."

- Old fat drunk man standing outside of a bar.

**Drink Thin. The new healthy lifestyle guide that teaches you how to maintain your figure (and your sex life) while boozing it up. Available now on Amazon.**

ElishaC Photography

WWW.ELISHAC.WEBS.COM
ELISHACPHOTOGRAPHY@GMAIL.COM

NOT ALL SNUS
IS CREATED EQUAL.

SWEDISH SNUS

*General*®

NORDIC MINT
15 PORTIONS

WARNING: This product can
cause gum disease and
tooth loss.

Made and imported from Sweden, General® Snus is 100% authentic
Swedish snus, with the quality, flavor and full-on tobacco satisfaction that make it
the #1 selling snus in the world. See why not all snus is created equal.
Go to **GeneralSnus.com** for special offers and more.

*General*®
THE ORIGINAL SWEDISH SNUS®

WARNING: This product can cause
gum disease and tooth loss.

# Hey Kids! Free Puke!

**Help Sell THE SNUFF TAKER'S EPHEMERIS** to all of your friends, enemies, family, teachers and clergymen! They'll love our articles and beg to buy more. Why, you could make dozens of dollars if you just work 20 hours a day until you hit puberty and realize how stupid this whole thing was!

## IMITATION VOMIT

Amazingly realistic PUKE! Looks like someone was SICK, SICK, SICK! almost turns your stomach to use as joke, it's so realistic. Made of plastic. The "gloppiest" look. Place by baby, dog, dinner table or pretend you've been sick. Most revolting, dirtiest trick we've seen. (Created a riot when we tested it!)

No. 2836. Price Postpaid. . . . . . . . . . . . . . . **50¢**

**Here's How It Works:**

You send us 398.00 and we'll send you a box of 40 magazines. Somehow you get other people to buy each copy for more than you paid for it. Then you send us a check or money order for 398.00 and we'll send you the FREE VOMIT (a .50 value). That's right- you get to KEEP ABOUT 2.00 (total may vary depending on how successful you are) and a piece of fake vomit (a 50 Cent Value!) Absolutely FREE! (Minus the upfront $398 cost of the magazines. NON- REFUNDABLE.)

So when your parents ask you why you've been up for days, shaking badly and walking into walls, just show them that it's because YOU want to be a SELF-MADE man by selling the STE like a REAL businessman. Instead of playing with your friends, you'll be out every day trying to turn an impossible profit. No tricks, no gimmicks, just good old-fashioned door to door rejection.

☐ I'm a stupid kid who just stole 400 bucks out of my mom's purse and I can barely read or write, much less do math. Please send me a stack of magazines I'll never end up selling.

☐ I'm not an idiot. I want to subscribe to your magazine and take advantage of all the good deals like quantity discounts and free shipping. I'm going to www.STEphemeris.com to find the subscription package that suits me best.

# Parting Shot

"Tobacco is my favorite vegetable."

-Frank Zappa

# STE®

© 2013 Lucien Publishing
Fayetteville, NC

Member: Independent Publisher's Trade Guild of North Carolina
"Providing Readers With Books That Matter"

www.ingramcontent.com/pod-product-compliance
Lightning Source LLC
Chambersburg PA
CBHW081542040426
42448CB00015B/3192